THE ROBIN HOOD COMPANION

by

Ronan Coghlan

BANGOR
(Co. Down):

XIPHOS BOOKS

2003

© Ronan Coghlan 2003

First Edition

Published by:

Xiphos Books,
1, Hillside Gardens,
Bangor,
Co Down,
BT19 6SJ,
NORTHERN IRELAND.

Introduction

When first we hear of bold Robin Hood, he is already established as a legend. We are told about a man who knew rhymes concerning our hero in Langland's *Piers Plowman* (1377). Here this reciter also knew rhymes of Randolf, Earl of Chester. The latter is certainly an historical character, but this does not necessarily make Robin Hood one, for rhymes can grow up about fictitious as well as factual persons. Did Robin begin as a ballad hero or a hero of the May Games? Is he someone with a real historical origin, the figment of some writer's imagination or perhaps even a mythological being hiding under a mantle of historicity?

In the first part of our work, these and other questions will be addressed in dictionary format. We shall also be looking at versions of his story that have appeared in novels, plays, operas, pantomimes, comics and on screen. Here a certain selectivity necessarily obtains. For example, the three television series *Robin Hood* (Sapphire Films), *Robin of Sherwood* and *The New Adventures of Robin Hood* have all attained a certain cult status and consequently have more entries devoted to them than more obscure works. The Robin Hood legend continues to grow and many such pieces have added considerably to the general public conception of Robin Hood.

The second part of the work consists of a translation into Modern English of the nearest thing approaching a Robin Hood epic, *A Little Gest of Robin Hood.* This, in many respects, provides something of a framework for his career. We do not know who wrote it or when exactly it was written. It has been suggested that, to produce it, the author took a number of ballads and melded them together; but, using other studies, we know that such works are not usually produced in such a manner. Writers such as the author of the *Gest* tend to know the stories of certain ballads, but to use their own words in retelling them in combined form. 1500 or thereabouts may be a good guess for the date of this poem. The first printed version we have was produced at Antwerp around the year 1510. No manuscript survives.

The mystique of the outlaw is something that has always attracted the public. Robin may be the best known of outlaw heroes, but he is far from being the only one. Ballads of such men are extremely popular and even if the outlaw in question was a scoundrel of the deepest dye in reality, popular imagination can quickly clothe him in the vestments of the hero. In reality, for most of history, the great mass of humanity has been downtrodden and arguably it still is. The appeal of a hero who despoils the rich, pits himself against tyranny and gets away with it most of the time can be discerned readily. Moreover, outlaws tend to have exciting adventures and these exploits provide that escapism on which the human imagination thrives.

If the reader has no great knowledge of Robin Hood, he is advised to commence by reading the article on Robin himself in the first part of the work. From there he can betake himself in whatever direction he chooses. The pathways of the legend are as twisted and labyrinthine as those of the forest itself and it is the author's hope that by treading them the reader will find both amusement and instruction. Insofar as I am aware, no work quite like this exists anywhere else and should make obscure material accessible to those needing to research the legend.

To conclude, the author would like to express his gratitude for assistance from Jonathan Downes and Tom Perrott.

Abbreviations referring to Robin Hood works cited in the text.

AD *Robin Hood and Alan-a-Dale* (ballad)
B *Robin Hood and the Bishop* (ballad)
BBVM *Robin Hood's Birth, Breeding, Valour and Marriage* (ballad)
BH *Robin Hood and the Bishop of Hereford* (ballad)
BP *Robin Hood and the Bold Pedlar* (ballad)
BRH *Birth of Robin Hood* (ballad)
CF *Robin Hood and the Curtal Friar* (ballad)
DeathREH Antony Munday *Death of Robert Earl of Huntingdon* (play)
DownfallREH Antony Munday *Downfall of Robert Earl of Huntingdon* (play)
GA *Robin Hood and the Golden Arrow* (ballad)
Geste *A Little Geste of Robin Hood* (poem)
GG *Robin Hood and Guy of Gisborne* (ballad)
GP *Robin Hood's Golden Prize* (ballad)
JPW *Jolly Pindar of Wakefield* (ballad)
KD *The King's Disguise and Friendship with Robin Hood* (ballad)
LJ *Robin Hood and Little John* (ballad)
LS Ben Gaultier *A Lay of Sherwood Forest* (poem)
MM *Robin Hood and Maid Marian* (ballad)
NARH *New Adventures of Robin Hood* (television series)
NF *Noble Fisherman* (ballad)
PA *Robin Hood and the Prince of Aragon* (ballad)
Parker Martin Parker *Life of Robin Hood* (biography)
PN *Robin Hood's Progress to Nottingham* (ballad)
QK *Robin Hood and Queen Katherine* (ballad)
RB-1 *Robin Hood and the Beggar* [first ballad] (ballad)
RB-2 *Robin Hood and the Beggar* [second ballad] (ballad)
RHB *Robin Hood and the Butcher* (ballad)
RHC *Robin Hood's Chase* (ballad)

RHD	*Robin Hood's Death* (ballad)
RHDel	*Robin Hood's Delight* (ballad)
RHGP	*Robin Hood's Golden Prize* (ballad)
RHLJ	Pierce Egan *Robin Hood and Little John* (novel)
RHM	*Robin Hood and the Monk* (ballad)
RHP	*Robin Hood and the Potter* (ballad)
RHS	*Robin Hood and the Shepherd* (ballad)
ROS	*Robin of Sherwood* (television series)
RSc	*Robin Hood and the Scotchman* (ballad)
RT	*Robin Hood and the Tanner* (ballad)
RWS	*Robin Hood Rescuing Will Stutely* (ballad)
SS	Ben Jonson *The Sad Shepherd* (unfinished play)
T	*Robin Hood and the Tinker* (ballad)
VK	*Robin Hood and the Valiant Knight* (ballad)
WTS	*Robin Hood Rescuing the Widow's Three Sons* (ballad)

A

ABBOTTS BROMLEY HORN DANCE A folk dance held annually in the Staffordshire village of Abbotts Bromley. It was originally a pagan fertility dance, but was taken under the wing of the Church and is now held on the Monday after the first Sunday after September 4th. The dancers wear reindeer antlers. One of them plays Maid Marian. She is always portrayed by a man and D. Pickford argues that as a man/woman she represents sexual commerce. The dance also features a boy with a bow and arrows, perhaps originally intended to be Robin Hood. The fertility nature of the dance is shown by the fact that the archer kills a hobby horse which is then revived, symbolising death and rebirth, just as the sown seeds of the dead (harvested) crops regrow in spring.

ADAM 1 A scholarly youth who helped Robin defeat the Sheriff in Moses Goldberg's play *The Outlaw Robin Hood* (1967).
2 A son of Robin by Elena, wife of the Sheriff of Nottingham in David Stuart Ryan's *The Lost Journal of Robin Hood-Outlaw* (1989).

AEGLAMOUR The Sad Shepherd of Ben Jonson's unfinished play of the same name. He loved Earine, whom he believed drowned in the River Trent. Actually, she had been kidnapped by the witch Maudlin and imprisoned in a tree. She intended him for her son. In a melancholic state, Aeglamour attended a feast given by Robin and Marian for the shepherds. They tried to cheer him up, but this was more than their ministrations could achieve. They themselves were to become involved with Maudlin later in the play.

AGNES The mother of Robin in Theresa Tomlinson's *The Forestwife* (1993). She had been the nurse of Mary de Holt, who became Marian. In the forest she became a healer, an herbalist and wisewoman, and passed on her lore to Marian.

AILRIC Father of Robin in ROS. He was the guardian of the symbol of pre-Christian religion, the Silver Arrow. During an uprising, he was killed by the Sheriff of Nottingham.

ALAN-A-DALE In the ballad which bears his name, Alan was seen by Robin one day, brightly clad and singing a roundelay. But next morning, when Robin saw him once more, gone was his *joie-de-vivre:* he looked desolate and downcast. He told Robin that the girl he had intended to marry had now been betrothed by her father to a groom well stricken in years. Alan agreed to be Robin's follower if the matter could be rectified. Robin turned up at the church on the wedding day disguised as a harper.. A bishop was to officiate at the nuptials. When bride and groom entered, Robin sounded his horn and his men appeared. With this armed band behind him, Robin said Alan should marry the bride. The bishop protested that the banns had not been called three times as was required. Little John then called them, not three, but seven times and Alan and the bride were married, Robin giving her away. According to tradition, the church where this wedding took place was at Dale Abbey, Derby. Alan is called Alan of the Dales in Jennifer Roberson's novels.

The name of the bride is traditionally given as Ellen; but in Henry Gilbert's *Robin Hood* (1914) she is called Alice. In Charles Gilson's *Robin of Sherwood* (1960) Alan fell in love with Marian, who in this version of the tale was Robin's sister. In ROS the bride is called Mildred. In RHLJ the story is adapted: Christabel is the young woman,

Allan Clare her swain and the Baron of Nottingham her father. Marian is Allan's sister. In Clayton Emery's *Tales of Robin Hood* (1988), Alan was a pacificist. His wife was called Elaine, as was his daughter. His son was Allan (so spelled) the Younger. He was skilled upon the harp and some of the songs he uttered were of a prophetical nature.

In the Sloane *Life of Robin Hood* (ca. 1600) the bridegroom of the tale is not Alan but Will Scarlet ("Scarlock").

ALBION This was the old Celtic name for Britain, surviving as Irish *Alba*, Scottish Gaelic *Alban* (Scotland). In ROS , it was one of the seven swords forged by Wayland the smith. It came to Robin to use in his role of the Hooded Man. His father Ailric had borne it before him, it had then fallen into the hands of the Sheriff of Nottingham, but Robin at last retrieved it.

ALFRED DE HUNTERTON J.Lees says that a Staffordshire headmaster (whose name he does not furnish) had a theory that Alfred de Hunterton, who revolted against Henry II and then became an outlaw in Cannock Chase Woods, was in fact the original Robin Hood. Although he robbed the rich, he saw no necessity to encumber the poor with the fruits of his depredations. The Sheriff he opposed was not him of Nottingham but rather him of Staffordshire, who was the Bishop of Lichfield.

AMAZONS The Amazons were a race of warrior women who once attacked Athens in classical mythology. In NARH they were introduced into the Robin Hood legend as Eleanor of Aquitaine recruited a troop of them as her supporters in the Holy Land and brought them back to England. Their leaders were called Selia and Alia.

ANEMONE This plant, in days gone by, was sometimes called "Robin Hood, Scarlet and John" after the outlaws.

ANGELINA In MacNally's opera *Robin Hood* (1784), she, disguised as a man, accompanied her cousin Clorinda to join Robin's band. Angelina's true love, Edwin, had departed on Crusade, but she did not know he had returned and was now living as a hermit in Sherwood, with Robin's permission. Luckily, she happened upon him by accident and they were reunited.

ANIMALS IN CARTOONS The use of cartoon animals to play characters in the Robin Hood saga reached its apogee in the Disney cartoon version of *Robin Hood*. Here Robin and Marian were foxes, King Richard and Prince John lions and Little John a bear. It is unfortunate that Friar Tuck in the form of a badger was depicted as the American rather than the English species. A new character, whose voice was delightfully rendered by Terry-Thomas, was Sir Hiss, a snake, Prince John's adviser,
This was not the first time cartoon animals assumed the personae of the legend. A short Warner Brothers cartoon featured Daffy Duck as an inept Robin Hood and Porky Pig as Friar Tuck, with hilarious results. This appeared in 1952. And we should not, perhaps, forget Bugs Bunny's appearance as *Rabbit Hood* (1949). *See also* **Robin Hoodnik.**

ANNA A member of Robin's band, enamoured of him, in the play *Robin Hood-the Legend of Sherwood* (2000) by R. Akers and J.D. Mesar.

ANNETTE In MacNally's opera *Robin Hood* (1784), the maidservant of Angelina, whom she accompanied in male guise when the latter went to join Robin's band.

ANNIE HOOD In RHLJ, the unfortunate sister of Gilbert Hood, Robin's adoptive father. The rapscallious Roland Ritson contracted a false marriage with her before a bogus priest and later murdered her. The bogus priest became an outlaw and one day Annie's ghost appeared to him. The apparition was seen also by Little John and Will Scarlet. The quondam pseudo-cleric was in a bad way before this encounter, for he had recently been thoroughly trounced with a quarterstaff and had had his ear bitten off by a dog. Seeing the ghost of Annie was the last straw and he perished by his own hand.

ANTICLERICALISM There is certainly a large element of anticlericalism in the Robin Hood saga, Robin urging his men to beat and bind bishops and archbishops, the depiction of the Abbot of St Mary's, of the Monk, of the Bishop of Hereford, etc. This doubtless reflected popular experience of certain unsavoury clerics. However, the sentiment is not universal. In the *Gest*, while the Abbot is shown heartless and grasping, the Prior evinces a much more Christian attitude.

Robin's personal religion, on the other hand, is profound. He does not like to miss Mass for long – indeed the *Gest* tells us he would hear three Masses a day before dining
and he has a strong reverence for the Virgin Mary. The latter is not to be seen as some kind of codeword for a pagan goddess, for this would completely negate the joke in the *Geste* in which, when Robin is waiting for the Virgin to pay him back the loan he made to Sir Richard, he takes it from the High Cellarer of St Mary's Abbey.

How then do we explain the difference between Robin's Christianity and his dislike of the clergy? The answer would seem to be that Robin or those who composed the tales about him were sufficiently sophisticated to distinguish between the Christian religion itself and those ministers of that religion who did not reflect its tenets in their lives.

ARAGON, PRINCE OF In PA, a Muslim potentate determined to wed the Princess of England, with whose name we are not favoured. With this in view, he besieged London. It was agreed between him and the King that, on a certain day, three English champions would fight three Aragonese and the Princess would fall to the victorious side. The Aragonese team was to consist of the Prince himself and two giants, which daunted the English so that no champions were to be found and it seemed the King must forfeit his daughter. Then Robin, Little John and Will Scarlet (here called Scadlock) turned up to take the English side. Robin was no whit abashed by some name calling on the Prince's part ("Fool! Fanatic! Baboon!") and in the ensuing fight slew him. Little John killed one of the giants and Scarlet the other. The King, discovering Robin's identity, offered him a pardon. As he could not divide his daughter into three parts and polyandry being unfashionable in medieval England, she was allowed to choose which outlaw she would wed. She chose Scarlet.

ARCHWAY HOUSE In Sherwood, a folly built in 1842. Statues of Robin Hood, Maid Marian, Alan-a-Dale and Richard the Lionheart embellish it,

ARLINGFORD, BARON OF Marian's father in Peacock's *Maid Marian* (1822). He is presented as a man of ill temper.

ARTHUR Legendary King of Britain, who may have thriven in the 6th Century. In NARH Merlin the wizard brought Robin and Rowena back to Arthur's time to help frustrate the designs of the Black Knight to seize Excalibur. In T.H. White's *The Sword in the Stone* (1938), Arthur as a boy called Wart is made a contemporary of Robin, with whom he shares an adventure. In this, Robin is called Robin 'ood, short for Robin Wood. *See also* **Round Table.**

ARTHUR-A-BLAND The tanner of Tamworth, a member of Robin's band. He was related to Little John on his mother's side. He met Robin and they fought with staves, but, after two hours of combat, neither was the victor. Robin then asked Arthur to join his band and the latter accepted. Robin then winded his horn and Little John appeared and embraced his relation. Then, according to RHT, Robin took them both by the hands and they danced around the oak tree, singing:

> "And ever hereafter as long as we live,
> We three shall be as one.
>   The wood it shall ring and the old wife sing
>   Of Robin Hood, Arthur and John."

ASCENSION DAY This Church feast day was the day on which Robin Hood plays were performed in the Somerset town of Yeovil. The last one recorded was in 1577, with one John Dyer taking the hero's part.

AZEEM In the film *Robin Hood Prince of Thieves* (1991) a black Muslim whom Robin met on Crusade and who returned with him to England and became a member of his band.

B

BABES IN THE WOOD The unhappy protagonists of a ballad printed in 1595. Their father being dead, their uncle commissioned two ruffians to murder them that he might have their inheritance. They were taken to the woods, but one of the men was unable to carry out so cruel an enterprise. He fought with and slew his companion, abandoning the two children in the forest, where they perished during the night. Everything subsequently went wrong for the uncle, who ended his life in durance.

The ballad, whose story is perhaps ultimately of Italian origin, was set in Norfolk and the wood identified with Wayland Wood (called 'Wailing Wood'). The uncle's house was said to be nearby Griston Old Hall.

In later versions of the story it is given a happy ending, with the children surviving, and this occurs in pantomime versions, where Robin Hood saves the children. He may have been introduced because in the original ballad the children were covered with leaves by a robin. In some versions the uncle is none other than the Sheriff of Nottingham. In Doreen Moger's pantomime *Babes in the Wood* (2002), he is given the name of Badlot, lest any doubt his nature.

BALOR In NARH, a dark god whom Marian was to be forced to wed and to whom she was to bear a child. She refused. Robin had to procure the horn of a unicorn to free her from the spell under which she had been placed as a result of this refusal. Balor is taken from Irish mythology where, as Balor of the Evil Eye, he was slain of Lugh Lamhfhada.

BARNSDALE In days agone, this Yorkshire forest, to the north of Sherwood, was often associated with Robin Hood. In the Middle Ages it was 30 square miles in extent, stretching from Badsworth in the west to Askem in the east, from near to Doncaster in the north to the Vale of Went in the south. Almost at the beginning of the *Geste* we are told that Robin "stood in Barnsdale" and the saying "Robin Hood in Barnsdale stood" was well-known by 1429 and had the status of a legal maxim.

Nonetheless, Barnsdale in Yorkshire poses some problems when it comes to identifying it with the Barnsdale of Robin Hood. For example, it was never a very big forest, never a royal forest where deer were protected. True, the references to Sayles, Wentbridge and Watling Street in the *Gest* all indicate the Yorkshire Barnsdale, but it is always possible that the author made the identification and, familiar with the local geography, threw them in to gain verisimilitude.

J. Lees has argued that the original Barnsdale of the legend was Bryunsdale, an area of Sherwood Forest, at the junction of Day Brook and the River Leen, much closer to Nottingham. This would reconcile the Barnsdale tradition with that of Robin flourishing in Sherwood. While many argue that the Sherwood tradition is a later development of the legend, Sherwood is in fact associated with Robin in an earlier written source than any mention of Barnsdale.

S. Knight suggests that Barnsdale in Rutland was the place of Robin's career. It still exists. It was a royal forest and deer are yet to be found there. It lies 25 miles south-west of Nottingham. Nearby are to be found Robin Hood's Field (near Whitwell) and Robin Hood's Cave (near Hambleton). The lord of this area was, in Anthony Munday's time, the Earl of Huntingdon.

Bransdale, to the north of Barnsdale, has also been suggested as the site of Robin's exploits and even Barnetvale near London.

BARKLAY In NARH, he was at first an underling of Prince John. He later became an inventor and actually managed to construct a time machine, which survived into modern times and was used by his descendant, Elvis, to go back into Robin's era.

BARON OF NOTTINGHAM In RHLJ, the father of Christabel. His name was FitzAlwin and he is in the latter part of the book given the title of Sheriff of that city. The story of Alan-a-Dale is reworked in this novel, making Allan Clare the lover of Christabel, whose father intends her to marry an elderly opulent knight. The Baron was an inveterate enemy of Robin Hood, cowardly by nature, but he had somehow managed to acquire the reputation of a hero. The Baron was well able to fling insults. On one occasion, when he noticed his officer Lambie had burn marks on his face he exclaimed of it "I have long recognised it by its severe ugliness, but it now exceeds by far all I ever beheld. Speak, dolt! into what grimy grease barrel have you thrust it."

BARRWOOD A place in Yorkshire. J. Wilson, writing in 1741, noted that there was a little wood here in which, it was said, Robin Hood was born.

BASILIA Daughter of Robert Fitz Odo. If the latter was the original Robin Hood, as some have contended, then she would have been Robin Hood's daughter.

BEATRICE A noblewoman. Although she was the daughter of the evil Baron Braisse-Neuve, she became a friend of Marian in Charles Gilson's *Robin of Sherwood* (1960).

BEGGAR There are two ballads about Robin Hood and beggars. In RHB (1), riding a horse worth ten angels, Robin came upon a beggar whom he challenged to combat. The beggar had a staff, Robin a "nut-brown sword". Then, when his blood was flowing, Robin agreed to change clothes with the beggar. In this guise he discovered that three men were to be hanged for killing deer. He sounded his horn, the outlaws arrived and the prisoners were freed.

In RHB (2), Robin stopped a beggar and tried to rob him. The beggar with his staff knocked the stuffing out of

Robin. Three of Robin's men came by and found him in a woeful state. One remained with him, while the others pursued the beggar. They ambushed and disarmed him, making him a prisoner. They set off with him to take him to Robin. He offered them £100, which he said was in his cloak, to set him free. They released him while he took off the said garment. He produced a bag of meal which he shook into his captors' eyes. He then grabbed the staff and served them as he had served their leader. This ballad reflects well neither on Robin or his followers. Ritson opines that it might have been composed in Scotland. *See also* **Four Beggars.**

BEN BARREL A member of Robin's band, originally called Barley, in Clayton Emery's *Tales of Robin Hood* (1988).

BENEDICT AND ELVIRA Two Jewish children befriended by Robin in Pamela Meldikoff's *The Star and the Sword* (1965). They were fleeing from persecution and helped to deliver King Richard's ransom.

BERENGARIA Queen of England, consort of Richard I, died perhaps 1230. She was the daughter of King Sancho VI of Navarre and married Richard in 1191. She became the lover of Robin in Nicholas Chase's *Locksley* (1983). She also features in John Owen Smith's pantomime *Robin Hood* (1990). The frequently found belief that Berengaria never set foot in England is inaccurate.

BESS Marian's maid in the film *The Adventures of Robin Hood* (1938).

BESTWOOD LODGE An hotel in Bestwood Country Park (Nottinghamshire). It is noted for its statues of Robin Hood characters.

BETTRIS The wife of George-a-Green, the Pindar of Wakefield. In the play *George-a-Green* (1599), she was the daughter of Grime and George, not yet a member of Robin's band, wished to wed her. Grime refused his consent, thinking she could do better than a mere pindar. Wily, George's servant, smuggled her out of her father's house and King Edward and Wily so arranged things that at last consent was given.

BICKERTON A sheriff sympathetic to Robin in NARH. Although something of a comic figure, he is depicted as being not without ability.

BILLY A character in the British television comedy *Last of the Summer Wine*, claiming to be a descendant of Robin Hood. He is to be seen dressed in Lincoln green and using the sobriquet "The Hawk" flitting about the local woodlands.

BILLY BOW A character in the British comic *Walt Disney's Weekly* (now defunct). He was a boy who joined Robin's band and became its mascot.

BIRKLIES In a number of MSS Kirklees is so called in error.

BISHOP In the ballad B, Robin discerned a Bishop and his entourage approaching and, fearing capture, fled to the house of an old woman, to whom he had given shoes and hose in the past. Knowing that if he were accosted by the Bishop's followers he could not but be worsted, he exchanged clothes with the ancient dame and left, carrying her spindle. Little John, seeing him approach, thought he was a witch and was minded to shoot him, but Robin called out in time to prevent such a disaster. Meanwhile the

Bishop, who would clearly have benefited from the services of an optician, finding the crone in Robin's clothes, mistook her for him and arrested her. As they proceeded, the Bishop and his company were waylaid by Robin and his outlaws. They relieved the prelate of £500, tied him to a tree and made him sing Mass before letting him go, apparently making him sit backwards on his horse for the ballad says "and gave him the tail in his hand". While the Bishop's diocese is not mentioned, the Bishop of Hereford in the ballad QK complained that Robin once tied him to a tree and made him say Mass.

BISHOP OF THE BLACK CANONS The holder of this extraordinary ecclesiastical title is to be found in the film *The Adventures of Robin Hood* (1938). Here he helped to frustrate the designs of John to be crowned King of England.

BISHOP'S WOOD A location in Sherwood Forest which was pointed out as the place where Robin had robbed the Bishop of Hereford.

BLACK BARBARA A woman of evil bent in Antonia Fraser's *Robin Hood* (1955). Her inclinations did not prevent her from becoming enamoured of the outlaw.

BLACK BART A blacksmith, he was a member of Robin's band in Clayton Emery's *Tales of Robin Hood* (1988).

BLACK KNIGHT In Scott's *Ivanhoe* (1818) this was Richard I in disguise. He and Robin were actively involved in the siege of Torquilstone.

BLACK ROSE An evil outcast Amazon with botanically related magical powers in NARH. She tried to seize the

Amazon crown and captured Robin, but the outlaws put an end to her designs.

BLACKBEARD A companion of Robin Hood in the Toronto *Telegram* comic strip *Robin Hood and Company* which ended in 1931.

BLIDWORTH Here Marian was said to have waited for Robin to take her to Edwinstowe to marry her. Here also Will Scarlet was said to be buried.

BLOOD AND GUTS LANE This was said to have been the former name of a lane in Sherwood. Robin and Little John were said to have had their famous fight on the bridge near here, but the river it spanned has now dried up.

BLOODLETTING It was by the letting of blood that Robin Hood was said to have met his death. Bloodletting was formerly a common medical and veterinary practice. It was held that various illnesses were caused by a superabundance of blood. The cure was to remove some of this. If only a small quantity of blood were judged needful of removal a leech was used. For a larger quantity a vein was opened. Various versions of the Robin Hood legend have him bled by the Prioress of Kirklees or by a male cleric. The way in which he was killed was that they let too much blood out and he bled to death. In the case of the Prioress, here motive seems obscure, but her paramour, Roger of Doncaster, was involved.

BOB A servant in *Robin Hood-the Musical* who in due course became Robin Hood, his deeds being inspired by love of Marian. This musical was performed in Chicago in 2001, the story being by Adam Burke, the music by Brian Posen and Ranjit Souri and the lyrics by Aaron Barr.

BOLD JANE DOWNEY A female member of Robin's band in Clayton Emery's *Tales of Robin Hood* (1988).

BOLSOVER Legend relates that two men were sinking a mineshaft near here and came upon what appeared to be Robin Hood's cave containing bows and other artefacts. Also present was a skeleton with a crucifix. Above the skeleton was written, "These died that we might live. *Requiescat in pace.*" Below the inscription was a list of names finishing with, "I was the last, Michael Tuck." This incident was supposed to have occurred in the 1820s.

BOROUGHBRIDGE Site of a battle fought in 1322 in which rebels against Edward II were defeated. J. Hunter argued that Robin was one of these rebels and subsequently became an outlaw.

BOW The weapon most closely associated with Robin and his followers. By the late 13th Century the longbow had become a very powerful weapon and was used by the armies of Edward I (reigned 1272-1307). The longbows of this period were armour-piercing. There has been some question as to whether the longbow was used in England before this time, but this idea seems to be based on a misunderstanding. The so-called "short bow" used before this seems to have been merely a shorter type of longbow. The term longbow properly applied simply means a bow other than a crossbow. Thus the use of the longbow in Robin Hood legends does not necessarily place them after the accession of Edward I.

Yew was a favoured wood for making a bow. The arrows were generally made of ash or poplar, the feathers plucked from a goose. Longbows could fire far faster than crossbows, the Norman weapon.

BOW, ROBIN HOOD'S This was apparently kept as a relic at Fountains Abbey as Ray notes in his *Itineraries* (1760). However there is a bow today at Renshaw Hall known as Robin Hood's. This is said to have been moved from Kirklees Hall in the late 1600s.

BRACKEN A plant which has sometimes been known as Robin Hood's sheep.

BRADFIELD The parish where Roger Dodsworth (17th Century) claimed Robin Hood was born. It is situated in South Yorkshire.

BRADFORD A city of Yorkshire, visited by Robin and George in the play *George-a-Green* (1599). There was a custom there amongst the shoemakers that if you did not trail your staff on the ground, you had to fight them. George, seeing the disguised kings Edward and James doing this, determined to fight the shoemakers himself, rather than play the villiago. Because of his skill with the quarterstaff, he trounced a goodly bunch of them.

BRAISSE-NEUVE, ROBERT An evil Norman baron who opposed Robin in Gilson's *Robin of Sherwood* (1960).

BRAMBLE A sprite in Noyes' *Robin Hood* (1926). He made Shadow-of-a-Leaf lose his wits, that he might have access to the fairy world. This play also mentions an old man called Gaffer Bramble, who does not appear. It seems that the Miller, embarrassed by the physical pecularities of his son Much, told someone that old Bramble, the palsied, lame sexton, was actually Much's father. Gaffer Bramble, having heard, turned up full of a righteous wrath that caused his nose to waggle.

BRAND, RIGHT HITTING An outlaw, one of the members of Robin's band. He is mentioned in Ritson's *Life* of Robin Hood.

BRIDGE The well-known card game. David Bird's book *The Bridge Adventures of Robin Hood* (1995) features Robin and his followers in situations involving this card game.

BROOKS, LORD The killer of Robin's father in the Italian film *Robin Hood i Pirati* (1960).

BROWN DOWN This stands near Chard (Somerset). A couple of barrows are to be found here and are known as Robin Hood's Butts. Here Robin Hood and Little John are said to have played quoits. Each hero stood on a barrow and threw rings to the other. The barrows are ¼ of a mile apart.

BUTCHER A travelling purveyor of meat, on his way to Nottingham. His tale is told in two ballads, each called *Robin Hood and the Butcher*, the first existing only in fragmentary form. In one version, Robin was set upon by the Butcher's dog which he killed. Robin bought the Butcher's wares and went into Nottingham, where he sold them more cheaply than the professional butchers. Invited to dine with the other butchers, Robin said Grace and offered to pay for the meal. The Sheriff was present and asked Robin if he had any horned beasts for sale. Robin replied in the affirmative and brought the Sheriff into Sherwood, where the beasts proved to be deer, not cattle. Robin winded his horn, his men appeared and he relieved the Sheriff of £300 before sending him on his way.

C

CAMPION, RED A flower. It is sometimes locally known as "Robin Hood".

CAMPSALL A place near Pontefract (Yorkshire). According to one tradition, Robin and Marian were married there.

CARL HOOD A malevolent sprite in English folklore. Those who would argue for a mythological origin of Robin Hood might regard them as connected.

CECIL A disguised girl who became enamoured of Little John in Robin McKinley's *Outlaws of Sherwood* (1988).

CEDWYN A witch who was a member of Robin's band in Clayton Emery's *Tales of Robin Hood* (1988). Of Welsh origin, she lived with Gilbert of the White Hand. She turned herself into a giant cat to fight the magical boar unleashed on the forest by an evil witch named Taragal.

CHAIR, ROBIN HOOD'S In Brome's *Travels Over England* (1700), we read that such a chair was shown in Sherwood. Brome himself sat on the chair and had what was claimed to be Robin Hood's cap put on his head. He was then given the "freedom of the chair".

CHALTAM, ROBERT The original name of Robin in Lisa Croll Di Dio's novel *Sherwood Forest* (1999) where he becomes an important pagan cultic figure.

CHESTER, EARL OF The father of Robin in the film *Tales of Robin Hood* (1951).

CHILTERN HILLS A once quite lawless area containing a place called Maidenhead Thicket. In this is to be found

Robin Hood's Bower, which may indicate that there were once tales connecting Robin with this part of England.

CHRISTABEL In RHLJ, the daughter of the Baron of Nottingham. She was in love with Allan, of whom her father disapproved. Robin became embroiled in their problem when he saved them from attack in Sherwood. She was fairly typical of Victorian heroines, in that she suffered from an utter lack of backbone and was prone to swooning in moments of peril. Her story is based loosely on the tale of Alan-a-Dale.

CHRISTMAS In Darren Vallier's pantomime *Robin Hood Saves Christmas* (2001), the Sheriff's endeavours to put an end to Christmas festivities were thwarted by Robin. The idea for this pantomime may have come from a ridiculous line in the film *Robin Hood Prince of Thieves.*

CLARINDA Heroine of the opera *Robin Hood: a New Musical* (1751) in which Robin helped her to marry Leander against the desires of her father, Graspall, who wished her to wed the unappetising Glitter.

CLERK OF COPMANHURST Title applied to Friar Tuck in Scott's *Ivanhoe* (1818). It is also used of the Friar in RHLJ.

CLORINDA The "queen of the shepherds" in BBVM. This ballad says that when Robin met her in Sherwood, he was deeply impressed by her, especially when she shot a deer, "the fattest buck in the land". He offered her marriage and she accepted, but said she had first to go to Titbury Feast. Robin went there too. On the way he was attacked by eight yeomen who wanted to take the buck he was carrying, but he and Little John fought them off. In Titbury Robin and Clorinda were married and she went to live in the greenwood. Clorinda is a somewhat literary name. It was borne by characters in Fletcher's *The Faithful Shepherdess* (1610) and Tasso's *Jerusalem Delivered* (1675). This would argue that the author of the ballad had some education. He seems to know nothing of the Maid Marian tradition. However, Clorinda was to feature again as Robin's beloved in MacNally's opera *Robin Hood* (1784), where she showed herself to be tough and resourceful, a heroine not unlike the Marion of NARH.

CLUB MOSS This plant is sometimes called Robin Hood's Hat Band.

COAT OF ARMS According to H. Bett, Robin's coat of arms was gules two bands engrailed or.

COCK ROBIN It has been suggested that the rhyme *Who Killed Cock Robin?* is connected with Robin Hood and that both hearken back to a paganism in which Robin was a sacrificed god. However, no printed version of the poem exists before 1744 and the Robin in question may be Robert Walpole, whose government fell in 1742.

CRAGAMON, WHIP OF A magical whip which had fallen into the hands of Brand, a slave-dealer in NARH. Robin and Marian infiltrated one of his auctions and Marian managed to send it back to Druid Grove, whence it had come.

CRUSADE Some modern versions of the Robin Hood legend make him a crusader who returned to England. This has doubtless been inspired by the idea he was a partisan of Richard the Lionheart, defending his rights against Prince John, rather than a true outlaw. The Crusade in question would have been the Third Crusade, which was undertaken to win back cities in Israel conquered by the Muslims. The

Holy Roman Emperor Frederick Barbarossa took the Cross in 1188, but drowned in the River Saleph on his way to Israel.. His death so far from home led to the legend that he sleeps beneath a mountain in Germany, waking every hundred years to see if his country has need of him. The two most powerful leaders now were Richard I and Philip Augustus of France. Richard proved an able commander, but eventually realised that, if he conquered Jerusalem, he could not leave sufficient men to garrison it. Therefore, though he had captured Acre, he had to return to England and was captured by Duke Leopold of Austria, whom he had insulted, on the way, this leading to the necessity of his ransom. The Christian campaign was not unmarred by atrocity. There is no record of any Robin Hood-like figure taking part. The Crusade ended in 1192.

D

DANES The writer G.K. Smith has argued that the original stories of Robin Hood dealt with his fighting against the Danes and were set around the time of King Canute (reigned 1016-35). He regards his first exploit as his attack on the pirates at Whitby. He contends that the King Edward of the ballad was Edward the Confessor (reigned 1042-1066).

DANU In Lisa Croll Di Dio's novel *Sherwood Forest* (1999), she renounced her leadership of the forest pagans, passing it on to Marian. Her name is based on that of the Irish pagan mother goddess, Dana or Anu. Amongst the Britons she was known as Don, but there is no reason to think she was ever revered amongst the Anglo-Saxons.

DARNEL The original name of Little John in *Robin Hood an Opera* (1730).

DAVID OF DONCASTER A member of Robin's band mentioned in the ballad GA. Here he was suspicious of the Sheriff's archery contest, feeling it was a trap, but Robin scorned his advice to be cautious, thinking it cowardly.

DE BERKEM An evil Norman baron who opposed Robin in Stocqueler's *Maid Marian* (1849).

DEER These formed the main meat supply of the outlaws, according to tradition. There are two native species of English deer, the red (*Cervus elephas*) and the roe (*Capreolus capreolus*). A third species, the fallow (*Dama dama*) may have been deliberately introduced, but this is by no means certain. All three were to be found in England in the Middle Ages and would have been available for the outlaws' menu.

DEERING The daughter of Robin and the heroine of the film *Son of Robin Hood* (1958). She was involved in a design to prevent the overthrowal of Henry III by the Black Duke. Helped by the Earl of Chester, who pretended to be Robin's son, the Duke's dastardly design was defeated.

DE GREY, WILLIAM A 13th Century Sheriff of Nottingham, possibly the original of the one in the Robin Hood legend, as he is known to have been pursuing outlaws in 1266.

DE MONTFORD, SIMON He was the brother-in-law of King Henry III (reigned 1216-1272) and led a rebellion in 1265. In G.P.R. James' novel *Forest Days* (1843), Robin, called Robin of the Lees by Ely, commanded his archers. See also **Evesham**.

DEPE DALE Here, in Francis Peck's ballad *Robin Whood Turned Hermit* (1735), Robin retired from his outlawry, selecting St Dismas as his patron. This is, of course, at variance with other accounts of the end of Robin's career.

DERBY NED In LS, the leader of a group of outlaws whose band was joined by some of Robin's followers after Robin's death.

DERWENT A member of Robin's band who featured prominently in the Sapphire television series *The Adventures of Robin Hood* (1955-60). The idea for this name may have come from the fact that near the Derwent Dams in the Peak District is a moor called Robin Hood's Moss.

DETECTIVE FICTION Author Clayton Emery has produced a number of mystery stories set in Robin Hood's England, with Robin and Marian as the detectives. They are to be published in book form under the title *Mayhem and Mystery*.

DIANA Heroine of the musical *Robin Hood and the Free People of the Forest* by Tobin James Mueller. She persuaded the Merry Men to become freedom fighters against the tyranny of King John.

DICKON In ROS, one of the founder members of Robin's band. He was killed early in the series. Dickon is also the name of the narrator in Eugenia Stone's *Robin Hood's Arrow* (1948).

DONCASTER, SIR *see* **Roger of Doncaster.**

DUMMY A mute servant boy who, having been ill-used, fled to Sherwood where he encountered Robin and Marian in M. Furlong's *Robin's Country* (1955).

DUNCAN A blind retainer of the Locksleys in *Robin Hood: Prince of Thieves.* Also, in the Sapphire Films *Robin Hood* television series, an ebullient Scotsman with a girlfriend called Jessie.

E

EARINE The beloved of Aeglamour in Ben Jonson's *Sad Shepherd.* The witch Maudlin imprisoned her in a tree, hoping she would yield to the advances of her son Lorel or, failing that, that he would force himself upon her.

EDWARD II King of England 1307-27. Because he made a progress in the north country, it has been suggested that he was the "Edward our comely king" of the *Gest.*
However, although he was handsome enough, it must be borne in mind that he was not popular in the north of England, where the *Gest* originated.

EDWARD IV King of England 1461-71; deposed and then restored, 1471-83. The events in the play *George a Green* (anonymous, but possibly by Robert Greene) place George and Robin Hood in his reign. It has been suggested that the *Gest*, while not placing Robin so late, reflects the chaotic conditions that then existed and that the phrase "Edward our comely king" may have been inspired by the handsomeness of Edward IV.

EDWARD AELREDSON The original name of Robin Hood in Parke Godwin's novel *Sherwood* (1991). In this Robin's career is set at the time of the Norman Conquest

(1066). The saga continues in *Robin and the King* (1993), partially set in France.

EDWINSTOWE A village in Sherwood. Here it was said that Robin and Marian were wed outside the church door, in accordance with medieval custom.

ELAINE The name of both the wife and the daughter of Alan-a-Dale in Clayton Emery's *Tales of Robin Hood* (1988).

ELDRED A priest who was Friar Tuck's companion in RHLJ. He was of advancing years.

ELEANOR In Jennifer Roberson's *Lady of the Forest* (1992), she was the daughter of the Sheriff of Nottingham. She was in love with Alan-a-Dale. When the Sheriff surprised them, Alan was accused of rape, so that Robin had to rescue him.

ELEANOR (ELINOR) OF AQUITAINE Mother of Richard I. She was the daughter of William X, Duke of Aquitaine and married in 1137 Louis, later Louis VII of France. When she accompanied Louis on Crusade, unfortunate rumours circulated concerning her private life. In 1152 her marriage was annulled. She had two surviving daughters, Alix and Marie. Later in the same year she married Henry II of England , by whom she had Geoffrey, Henry, Richard and John. Henry, Richard and John rebelled unsuccessfully but with their mother's backing. As a result she was imprisoned for sixteen years. When Richard was on Crusade she acted as regent, opposed John's designs and helped raise money for Richard's ransom. Despite this, when John came to the throne, he held her in high esteem. She died in 1204.

In various versions of the Robin Hood stories set in Richard's reign, she has made an appearance. In NARH, the Disney live action *Robin Hood* and the Sapphire Films *Robin Hood* television series, she was featured.

In *DownfallREH* she, although well stricken in years, fell most inappropriately in love with Robin and even exchanged clothes with Marian with a view to seducing him. In *Robin Hood Comics* #5 (Quality Comics), there is a rehash of the ballads featuring Robin and Queen Katherine, but here Eleanor is substituted for Katherine.

ELENA *see* **Sheriff's Wife.**

ELINOR In Noyes' *Robin Hood* (1926), the sister of Prince John. When he was young, Robin had been her page and had fallen in love with her. She had rejected him. Later, she tried to win him from Marian and it was she, not the Prioress of Kirklees, who bled Robin to death. She also killed Marian.

ELY, BISHOP OF An historical person named William Longchamp who flourished in the reign of Richard I and was made joint justiciar during his absence. The people regarded him with much detestation. He was a strict ruler. Prince John and the barons rebelled against him in 1191. They then came to an agreement with him, but he was later deposed for arresting the Archbishop of York. By 1193 he was in Germany. He died in 1197. In *DownfallREH* Prince John showed him letters in which his power was transferred to John. The Bishop then plotted a rebellion, which was unsuccessful. He escaped from Prince John's clutches and made his way through the woodlands disguised as an egg seller. Robin, realising who he was, bought his eggs and found the royal seal amongst them. He then asserted that this venerable purveyor of eggs must have murdered the Bishop and stolen the seal, so the Bishop had to reveal his identity.

EOSTRA According to the Venerable Bede, this was the name of an Anglo-Saxon goddess, though doubts have been expressed regarding this. Phillips and Keatman suggest she is the original of the Maid Marian of the May Games and, indeed, if she existed, she would have been connected with the spring, though J. Grimm tried to link her with the dawn.

EPITAPH *see* **Robin's Grave.**

EVANS THE HALF HUMAN HAWK WOMAN The personage with this interesting name is to be found in the pantomime *The Legend of Robin Hood* by John Morris.

EVESHAM Site of a battle in Worcestershire fought in 1265. Simon de Montfort, brother –in-law of Henry III, had led an uprising to gain reforms, but the King's nephew, Prince Edward (later Edward I) crushed him at Evesham. It has been suggested that Robin and Little John had taken part in this battle on de Montfort's side and that they subsequently became outlaws. This is the period to which Walter Bower's extension of Fordun's *Scotichronicon* assigns to the outlaw.

F

FAIR MASTER In the musical *Arrow* (1995), this official was in charge of the annual fair to which Robin came to shoot.

FERN-WHISPER Queen of the Forest Sprites in Noyes' *Robin Hood.*

FIONA A princess in the animated film *Shrek* (2001). While she was being escorted by an ogre, Robin Hood mistook her guardian for her captor, tried to rescue her and would not be gainsaid, so she had to rid herself of the attentions of him and his Merry Men with some surprising martial arts skills which none had hitherto realised she possessed. For some reason in this production Robin is given a French accent.

FITZHERBERT, BARON In MacNally's *Robin Hood* (1784), the father of Robin's innamorata, Clorinda. He brought about her imprisonment, but she escaped to Sherwood.

FITZHOOD, SIR ROBERT The father of Robin in Robert and Caroline Southey's unfinished *Robin Hood; a fragment* (1847). He died on crusade.

FITZODO, ROBERT *see* **Locksley**.

FITZOOTH The surname of Robin Hood in Stukely's erroneous pedigree which made him Lord of Kime. However, R. Planche felt that Fitzooth might have been an error for FitzOdo, a family of Loxley in Warwickshire. The name Fitzooth came to be widely used in versions of the tale of Robin. In J. Walter McSpadden's *Robin Hood* (1904), Hugh Fitzooth, a forester, was Robin's father. In RHLJ, Robert Fitzooth, Earl of Huntingdon, was Robin's grandfather. He died, leaving him in the care of Philip Fitzooth, his brother, who wanted to seize the earldom. The son died as an adult, but not before fathering an heir, Robin Hood himself. Philip placed him for adoption with Gilbert Hood, his existence being kept a secret, thus enabling Philip to gain the earldom.

FITZOOTH, RALPH According to Stukeley's erroneous pedigree in *Palaeographia Brittanica* (1743-52), this was the original Robin Hood. He married Maud, daughter of Gilbert de Gant and Rohaise, daughter of William Fitzgilbert.

FITZWA(L)TER The name of Marian's father in *DownfallREH.* Prince John asked him to procure for him his daughter's favours. Enraged, Fitzwater attacked John and was banished. An inconsistency in the play makes Marian's father elsewhere Lord Lacy. Drayton also made Marian Fitzwalter's daughter and in subsequent versions of the tale Fitzwalter has become her surname. In Jennifer Roberson's *Lady of the Forest* (1992), his first name was Hugh and he wanted Marian to marry the Sheriff. In Gary Yershon's play *Robin Hood* (1996), he found Robin as an urchin of the streets and brought him up as a servant.

FLASK, ROBIN HOOD'S A leather flask, claimed to be Robin's, is in Southwell Minster Library. It is of 16th Century type. It was bequeathed by the Southwell family, amongst whom the tradition that it was Robin's is longstanding.

FLORA The Roman goddess of flowers (Latin *flos,* genitive *floris,* a flower). In the Maying which Henry VIII and Katherine of Aragon attended in 1515, she was present with Robin Hood and Lady May. Her turning up in England may not be due simply to classical learning. She is also found associated with the Cornish Furry Dance. She may have replaced an earlier figure such as Blodeuedd, a being from Celtic mythology made from flowers. Whatever her origins, it would seem to be her involvement in the May Games which associated her with Robin Hood.

FOREST LAWS These were the laws against hunting the King's deer in royal forests, which Robin and his followers often flouted. There were offences against vert (greenery) and venison (hunted meat). The Laws were eventually relaxed, so that one could not be executed for breaking them. Though the outlaw ballads as a whole respect the law itself, as distinct from its corrupt officers, they despise the Forest Laws as an affront to justice.

FORESTERS Officials or guardians whose duty it was to see that the Forest Laws were obeyed. They would have been opposed to an historical Robin Hood. Technically, there were three kinds of foresters:-

[a] foresters properly so-called, who upheld the laws against poaching;

[b] verderers cared for timber; and

[c] agisters connected with grazing rights in the forest.

FORESTWIFE The title given to Marian in books by Theresa Tomlinson. Marian became a healer in the forest by gleaning knowledge from a wise woman.

FOUNTAIN DALE A place which Friar Tuck had kept for seven years. It has been identified with Fountain Dale near Mansfield. East of it is to be found Friar Tuck's Well. It has been suggested that Friar Tuck was one of a series of hermits whose job it was to attend the well. These hermits may have been attached to the Augustinian priory of Newstead (sometimes miscalled an abbey) which was located in Sherwood. The river which Robin and the Friar crossed and recrossed may have been a moat surrounding a chapel and shrine. According to legend, Friar Tuck was thrown out of his cell by the Augustinians after seven years. The Augustinians put a curse on the well which dried up for seven years. Subsequently the water only flowed every seven years.

FOUNTAINS ABBEY This lies three miles south-west of Ripon (Yorkshire). Ritson claimed Robin's bow and arrow were kept there. This belief may have arisen because of a large bow and arrow engraved there. There is a Robin Hood's Well nearby.

FOUR BEGGARS The ballad LJB tells how Robin sent Little John to beg, which doesn't sit well with the tradition of the *Gest*, which has the outlaw band well in funds.
We are told that John encountered three other beggars, who tried to attack him. One was apparently dumb, but a blow from John's quarterstaff made him roar; another seemed to be a cripple, but proved to be able to walk, while a third, apparently blind, showed himself able to see. John flung these all too healthy mendicants against a wall and discovered they had £603 about them, in cloak and bag, and this sum he bore back to Robin.

FRIAR HARDY In a projected comedy film based on the Robin Hood legend, Oliver Hardy was to take this part, modelled on Friar Tuck, while Stan Laurel was to play Little John Laurel. For some reason the project never materialised.

FRIAR TUCK The jovial cleric of Robin's band. The story of Robin's meeting with him is given in two ballads, one incomplete. Informed of the Friar's prowess, Robin visited him and besought him to carry him on his back to the far side of a river. The Friar complied, but then forced Robin to carry him back at swordpoint. Robin then in like fashion compelled the Friar to carry him back once more. In midstream, Tuck dropped Robin into the water. Gaining the bank, Robin loosed arrows at the Friar, but the latter used his targe to protect himself until his antagonist's arrows were spent. They fought then with sword and buckler for six hours. Robin then entreated the Friar to let him wind his horn three times. The cleric acquiescing, Robin did so and fifty of his men appeared. The Friar, unfazed, asked permission to put his fist in his mouth and whistle three times or, as the ballad puts it, "whute whutes three". Fifty curtal dogs then turned up and set on Robin, ripping his Lincoln green mantle. The men then shot arrows at the dogs, but the resourceful canids seized them and kept them in their mouths. Little John unloosed shafts killing ten of the dogs and the Friar made peace with Robin and joined his band.

The story is also told in a 16th Century play *Robin Hood and the Friar*. This, which antedates extant versions of the ballads, was intended for using at May Games. In this drama, the Friar had earlier despoiled Robin of his purse. He has two followers, Cut and Bause, who replace the dogs. In fact, Tuck may have originated in the May Games, only later being incorporated into the Robin Hood mythos. The tale of the river fight has a variant in the Sloane *Life of Robin Hood* (*ca.* 1600). Here Robin's opponent was not Tuck but Much.

The Friar and his dogs are described as *curtal*, a somewhat mysterious word. It may mean the Friar's habit was cut short and his dogs' tales docked. F.G. Child suggested it is an anglicised form of Latin *curtilarius*, meaning 'tending the vegetable garden of the monastery', but this can hardly explain its application to the dogs, who were hardly envisioned as plying hoe and trowel. It was said that Tuck came from Fountains Abbey, but this was a Cistercian establishment which did not house friars. The first friars to enter England were the Dominican Friars or Friars Preachers, who arrived in 1221.

In *DownfallREH*, Friar Tuck was the confessor to the sons of the Widow Scarlet and helped Robin to rescue them. Peacock in *Maid Marian* (1822) says his name was Michael. This is probably taken from the Sloane MS, where he is called *Muchel.* In ROS at the beginning of the series he was the Sheriff's chaplain. In RHLJ he first met Robin when he sought shelter at the cottage of Gilbert Hood on a snowy night. In NARH he was something of a scientist and a visiting extraterrestrial helpfully informed him that the world was round.

The term "tuck" may have been applied to all friars because they wore a girdle that tucked in their habits. However, in England the Friar's name has come to be associated with *tuck*, 'food', hence contributing to his rotund – indeed Bunteresque – image.

Of the Friar John Taylor the Water Poet had this to say in *An Arrant Thief* (1623):

"Then Friar Tuck, a tall stout thief indeed,
 Could better rob and steal than preach or read."

In 1429 one Richard Stafford in the south of England used the nom-de-guerre of Frere Tuck in his criminal exploits. Is he the original of our portly friar, who seems to have been mentioned for the first time around 1475?

FRIAR TUCK'S BOW A bow in fact of comparatively recent origin, which was lent to the owner of Fountain Dale House. A tradition grew up that the weapon was the portly friar's.

FRIAR TUCK'S DAUGHTER In the Japanese play *Robin Hood* (1927) by Tomoyoshi Maryamu, the Friar had originally been a cobbler. His wife died, leaving him with a daughter. Later, he entered the religious life. His daughter was a fierce virago, in love with the Sheriff of Nottingham. She drove away his unfortunate wife and married him herself. Her antics at length drove the unhappy Friar to commit suicide.

FRONT DE NOIR In RHLJ a servant of the Baron of Nottingham. He was sent to murder Allan Clare by his master. When Allan was senseless and he was digging a hole with a view to burying him, Friar Tuck happened upon him. A fight ensued and Tuck killed him with a quarterstaff.

FULK FITZWARIN An historical person, born between 1170-80, died *ca.* 1255. The subject of a romance, he is mentioned here because he was an outlaw and it has been argued that his career was one of the components which made up the eventual saga of Robin Hood.

Historically, he became an outlaw by a miscarriage of justice in 1200. He had been Lord of Whittington (Shropshire) since 1197, but a rival had seized it, enjoying the support of King John. He led a guerrilla campaign against King John from 1200-1203. Then he was pardoned and Whittington Castle restored to him. He rebelled again in 1215 and continued in arms until after John's death in 1217. In *DownfallREH*, Matilda, later known as Marian, had to flee from King John's embraces by going to the forest. In much the same way Fulk's wife Maude had to join her husband in his outlawry because John was enamoured of her. It should be noted the name Maude is a variant of Matilda.

The romance of *Fulk Fitzwarin* has a number of surprising parallels with the *Gest.*
Just like Robin, Fulk had a henchman called John, in this case his brother; in the *Gest* Little John takes service with the Sheriff and brings him as a prisoner to Robin. In *Fulk Fitzwarin*, John does exactly the same thing with Fulk's enemy, Sir Morice. King John is captured by Fulk's men and promises he no longer will harass the outlaws, then

going back on his word. Exactly the same scenario occurs when Robin captures the Sheriff. In addition, in the first mention we have of Robin (*Piers Plowman*), ballads of Robin are coupled with those of Randolf, Earl of Chester. This worthy actually occurs in the Fulk romance: King John sends him against Fulk, but he ends up by joining Fulk's band. The present form of the *Gest* was not written until about 300 years after *Fulk Fitzwarin.*

As a curious postscript, there is a song called *Robyn and Gandelin.* The Robyn is not intended to be Robin Hood, but is slain by one Wrennock. Surprisingly, Wrennock is the name of the son of Fulk's supplanter, Sir Morice of Powys.

G

GAMBOL GREEN A pedlar who, in BP, was waylaid by Robin and Little John. John demanded half his pack. The pedlar refused. He and Robin had a sword fight. After a time, Robin halted this identifying himself and Little John and the pedlar did likewise, saying he was Gambol Green who had had to flee overseas, because he had killed someone. Robin now realised that he was his (Robin's) nephew and

> "They went to the tavern and there they drink
> And crack'd the bottle most merrily."

Gambol Green must be identical with Will Scarlet as their stories match and Gamwell was supposed to be Scarlet's real surname.

GAMELYN Hero of a romance called *The Tale of Gamelyn* (?14th Century), it has been suggested that in Gamelyn we have the origin of the name Gamwell borne by

Robin's relations, especially Will Scarlet(=young Gamwell). In E.M. Buckingham's *Robin Hood* (1905), he and Scarlet are identified.

GAMWELL Robin's uncle who lived in Great Gamwell Hall. In BBVM he besought Robin to stay with him, giving him Little John as a page. Will Scarlet's real surname was Gamwell. In RHLJ, Little John was the nephew of Sir Guy Gamwell. With regard to the actual existence of a Gamwell family in the Middle Ages, Camden avers there was one in Yorkshire. At the time of the Norman conquest (1066), there was a Gamel living in Nottinghamshire, a possible progenitor of this family. The character of Robin's uncle may have been inspired by Sir William Holles, who was called the Good Lord of Haughton (died 1590). In RHLJ there features a ferocious battle between Norman and Saxon when the former attack Gamwell Hall.

GARLANDS Collections of Robin Hood ballads in printed form. These booklets, published from 17th-19th Centuries, could contain as many as a hundred pages. The first garland we have was called simply *Robin Hood's Garland* (1663).

GASPAR-A-TIN In RHLJ this is the name given to the Tinker in the ballad T who was a member of Robin's band.

GEOFFREY DE MANDEVILLE According to Stukely's inaccurate pedigree of Robin Hood, he was Robin's grandfather and himself something of a plunderer. He had supported the Empress Matilda in her war with King Stephen (reigned 1135-54). Stephen confiscated sundry of his properties, after which he became a freebooter.

GEORGE-A-GREEN The Pindar of Wakefield who became a member of Robin's band. Originally he was a pindar, i.e., one whose duty it was to impound stray cattle. He challenged Robin, Little John and Scarlet when they crossed a cornfield where they had no business to be. In the combat which ensued, the outlaws' swords were all broken and Robin, impressed with the Pindar's prowess, offered him a place in his band. George said he would join Robin when his contract had expired.

The local village of Stanley is supposed to be where the fight took place. Another suggestion, mooted in 1864 in *Notes & Queries,* is Robin Hood Hill in Wrenthorpe near Wakefield.

George was perhaps originally a separate local hero, being only latterly drawn into the Robin Hood cycle. The story given above is related in JPW, published in the 17th Century, but the background story appears to have been in existence as least as early as the 16th. George was the hero of the play *George-a-Green* (printed 1599), perhaps by Robert Greene. Here George opposed the rebellious Earl of Kendal and Robin is a comparatively minor character. In his original legend, George is said to have run off with the daughter of a Justice Grymes. He may have been drawn into the ambit of Robin Hood from the May Games.

A modern poem in Yorkshire dialect *Robin Hood a Yorkshireman* by Bert Greensmith, replaces Little John with George at the fight with Robin on the bridge which he claims spanned Bushy Beck at Top at Wood (now Kirkhamgate).

GILBERT DE HOOD In *DownfallREH*, Robin's uncle and the Prior of York. He wished to see Robin outlawed and managed to accomplish this with small difficulty, for Robin owed him money he could not repay.

GILBERT HOOD (His name is also written *Head*). Robin's adoptive father in RHLJ. His siblings hadn't much luck. His twin brother was slain by an outlaw and buried beneath an oak tree, while his sister was murdered by Roland Ritson, a villain who went on to grow old in skulduggery.

GILBERT WITH THE WHITE HAND One of Robin's band. He attended the archery contest in the *Geste.* In one text he is called Gilbert of the Lily-white Hand. P.V. Harris has traced a medieval family of Withehondes to which he feels Gilbert might have belonged. Emery's *Tales of Robin Hood* (1988) makes him a Scottish knight, cohabiting with the pagan witch Cedwyn.

GODIVA In NARH, a witch whom Robin had imprisoned in a tree. When she later escaped, she captured Robin, who then had to be rescued by women, as men were too susceptible to Godiva's charms.

GOLDEN ARROW In the ballad GA, the Sheriff proclaimed an archery contest, the prize to be an arrow with a silver shaft and a golden head. He was sure Robin would enter and be trapped. Robin and his men arrived and mingled with the crowd, so they were not discerned by the watchful magistrate. Robin won the Golden Arrow, but overheard the Sheriff saying Robin Hood had not dared to turn up.

Back in the forest, Robin was very anxious that the Sheriff should know he had attended the competition. Little John suggested they write the Sheriff a letter informing him of this. This missive was shot on an arrow into Nottingham and in due course delivered to the addressee. The Sheriff was not pleased:

"And when he read, he scratch'd his head

And rav'd like one that's mad."

GOLDEN PRIZE In the ballad GP, Robin disguised himself as a friar and begged money from two priests. The priests claimed they had no money on them, so Robin made the them kneel with him to pray for some. Any money they found they had at the end of their orisons was to be divided up amongst them. After their prayers, Robin searched them and found they had much gold upon them, of which he cheerfully took a third, claiming that heaven had answered their pleas. Despite the fact that they had apparently been on the receiving end of a miracle, the priests do not seem to have felt in any way uplifted by the experience.

GRAVE, ROBIN HOOD'S Grafton claimed the Prioress of Kirklees had buried Robin Hood in a grave beside the road. At either end of the place of burial was a cross, which Grafton averred could be seen in his day. The gravestone bore the names Robin Hood, William of Goldsborough and others. Elsewhere we learn that the name Thomas also appeared on it.

Sir Samuel Armytage had the ground dug up to a depth of a yard, but found it had never been disturbed. Surprisingly, the grave of Constance Cove Jones, buried in the 19th Century at Loxley in Warwickshire has a gravestone bearing a striking resemblence to the one at Kirklees drawn by Nathaniel Johnston in 1665. Various versions of the epitaph on the stone exist. In Martin Parker's *True Tale of Robin Hood* it runs as follows:

Robert, Earl of Huntingdon,
Lies underneath this little stone.
No archer was as he so good.
His wildness named him Robin Hood.
Such outlaws as he and his men

May England never see again.

A variant of the epitaph was supplied by Thomas Gale, Dean of York 1697-1702:

Here underneath this little stone
Lies Robert Earl of Huntingdon.
No archer were as he so good;
The people called him Robin Hood.
Such archers as he and his men
Will England never see again.

Whatever the wording of the inscription, Thoresby, writing in the 18th Century, said by then it was "scarce legible". Thomas Gent in 1730 said there was a tombstone that actually bore an effigy there – of Robin presumably.

In recent times paranormal activity has been reported around the grave. An apparition of a woman has been seen there as has one of a person in a white robe. (The two are perhaps identical). Investigator Barbara Green claims she saw the ghost of Red Roger there, but admits this may have been an hallucination. It has also been suggested that there has been vampire activity in the vicinity. Mrs. E. Ellis, in the early part of the 20th Century, claimed to have seen silver arrows above Kirklees and to have heard Robin calling for Marian. A farmer claimed to have been sitting on the gravestone in 1926 when he was tapped by an invisible entity. His shotgun went off and the recoil knocked out two of his teeth.

Another Robin Hood's Grave is to be found in Cumbria. It is marked by a cairn.

A 13th Century grave at Hartshead in Yorkshire has also been claimed as the bold outlaw's.

A legend discovered by R. Rutherford-Moore says that, after Robin died, his followers buried him in a secret grave.

They were afraid the authorities would abuse the body in retaliation for his activities.

GRAY, EARLIE A follower of Robin who remained with Little John after Robin's death in LS.

GREEN ARROW An American comic book hero who bore a distinct resemblance to Robin Hood in that he was an archer, defeating his foes with different kinds of arrows. He first appeared in National Comics *More Fun Comics* #73 (1941). He was created by Mort Weisinger. His exploits were set in modern times and he was modelled on Batman, even to the extent of having a boy companion named Speedy. As the stories about him grew, it was revealed that he was a descendant of Robin Hood. Robin, who in this series claimed to be a son of Herne, had himself a secret son, Sir Robert Queen, an ancestor of Oliver Queen who became Green Arrow in the 20th Century. In one story Green Arrow's partner-in-crimefighting, Black Canary, was whisked back through time and entered Marian's body.

GREEN MAN A name given to carved foliate heads in churches. These carvings are either bedecked in leaves or have leaves protruding from mouth or eye. The motif of such heads goes all the way back to Roman times and entered England only in the 12th Century. Lady Raglan argued that the Green Man represented the woodland spirit also known as Robin Hood, Jack in the Green or the King of the May. Her theory went far further than the evidence she produced would warrant. That Robin was some kind of forest spirit is far from clear, as the earliest sources for his adventures say nothing of magic or the supernatural. The further identification of the Green Man with the Green Knight of Arthurian legend is no more than speculation. The waters are further muddied by the fact the term Green

Man was formerly applied to the wodewose or wild man believed to inhabit English woodlands. D. Kennedy *England's Dances* (1950), however, argues that Robin was a primeval figure, a sort of medicine man, identified with the Green Man.

T. Molyneaux-Smith produced the interesting theory that foliate heads are those of outlaws whose heads were camouflaged with greenery. In the chapter house at Southwell Minster on the borders of Sherwood Forest, there are several foliate heads.

Many signs outside pubs called 'The Green Man' bear a picture of Robin Hood.

GRIME The father of Bettris. George-a-Green wished to marry her, but Grime opposed the match. Wily, George's servant, turned up on his doorstep disguised as a woman, to help Bettris escape. Unfortunately, his disguise was so effective that Grimes fell in love with him and said if he could have Wily, George might wed Bettris. He was not pleased when Wily's true gender was revealed.

GUY OF GISBORNE The opponent of Robin in the ballad which bears his name. In this, Robin had had a bad dream. He and Little John went into the woods and saw, leaning against a tree, a man in a horsehide garment, with mane attached. Robin and John had a disagreement and John went off in a huff. He came upon the Sheriff and two of his men killing outlaws. Two had already fallen and another, Will Scarlet, was fleeing into the distance. Little John let fly an arrow and transfixed a soldier, but then his bow broke and he was seized and tied to a tree.

Robin, meanwhile, had had an archery contest with the stranger in equine caparison. He had discovered that the latter was called Guy of Gisborne and he had been sent to hunt him down. When Robin revealed his identity, the two fell to fighting. Robin fell on a root, but managed to gain his feet again. He killed Guy and, in a rather savage episode, disfigured him with an Irish knife. He then donned Guy's strange raiment and, in this guise, happened upon the Sheriff. Little John was still tied to a tree. He told the Sheriff he had killed Robin and asked, if as a reward, he might slay the underling as he had slain the master. He drew near to John, cut him free and gave him Guy's bow. He opened fire and the Sheriff's men fled, but one of John's arrows killed the Sheriff. There is some evidence that there were separate tales of Guy of Gisborne which did not involve Robin, for William Dunbar (?1456-?1513) mentions him without any reference to the outlaw. His name comes from the village of Gisburn near the River Ribble.

In de Koven's opera *Robin Hood* (1890), Guy was Robin's half-brother, the child of a secret marriage by his father before Robin's birth. The Sheriff wished Guy to wed Marian, but his plans did not work out as expected. In modern screen versions of the saga, Gisborne figures more prominently than he did in the early tales, for example in the silent *Robin Hood* (1922). In *The Adventures of Robin Hood* (1938), Basil Rathbone gave a much admired performance of the character. In ROS, he was an upper class thug, in the humorous *Maid Marian and her Merry Men* an imbecile. He was a formidable knight in Emery's *Tales of Robin Hood* (1988), while in Catherine Todd's *Marian* (1991), Marian actually married him. He was probably the inspiration for the character Guy of Glamore in the ME Comics *Robin Hood* series.

GUY OF WARWICK Robin's maternal great uncle, according to BBVM. He was a celebrated character in medieval romance, having originally had no connection with our outlaw. He was credited with such deeds as killing the giant Colbrand. However, Guy was said to have lived in the time of the Saxon king Athelstan (reigned 925-

939), which would make him much too early for the relationship claimed in the ballad.

GWYN Daughter of Robin Hood in the Disney film *Princess of Thieves* (2001). With Richard the Lionheart dying, Prince John wanted to grab the throne from Prince Philip, the rightful heir, whose memory has not been preserved by historians. Robin and his men, trying to prevent this dastardly act, went into action but were captured, but Robin's 18-year old daughter Gwyn was ready to take the necessary steps to set things right.

GWYNETH In NARH, a healer, sent out by the god of healers in Avalon. She had to return thither by her twenty-first birthday, or all whom she had healed would die. Guy of Gisborne knew she had once saved Robin, so he tried to prevent her going back. However, Guy was killed by Robin and Gwyneth revived him. This meant he had to let her go home lest the effects of her healing be undone.

H

HAL AN TOW Verses sung during a walk around the town which form part of the traditional Furry Day at Helston in Cornwall. They contain references to Robin Hood and Little John. The festival celebrates the change from winter to summer.

HAL OF THE KEEP In RHLJ, the foster-brother of Maude. He often aided Robin.

HARLEQUIN The lead character of the Harlequinade, which generally appeared on the English stage around Christmas time. He wore a mask, a spangled costume and generally carried a wand or slapstick. He was adopted from the Italian *Commedia del'Arte*. He features as a character in Pearce's *Merry Sherwood* (1795). Here he was given to Robin as a guardian by the Witch of Nottingham Well and was much involved with the fantastic elements in the play.

HART OF GREECE In CF allusions are made to such a beast. A hart is generally a young stag, but in terms of venery a hart of Greece meant the biggest and plumpest kind of stag. The word *Greece* may be simply a corruption of 'grease'.

HARTSHEAD A place in Yorkshire containing a 13th Century grave. This grave is reputed to be Robin's. It is therefore a rival to the Kirklees grave.

HATHERSAGE Village in Derbyshire, said to be the birthplace and to contain the grave of Little John.

HAWES, BEN In LS, Little John's page.

HAY OF NAUCHTON The slayer of Gilbert of the White Hand in G. Douglas' *Palace of Honour* (pre-1518). The event took place in 'Madin Land'.

HENRY The king in the ballads RHC and RHD; for further information *see* KATHERINE.

HENRY II, King of England 1154-89. The father of Richard the Lionheart and Prince John, he rarely figures in connection with Robin Hood, but in the Elizabethan drama *Look About You* (1600), he is on the throne. Whether this piece should be described as a Robin Hood play is doubtful, for, though Robin features in the text, it is entirely as a nobleman, the Earl of Huntingdon. His outlawry goes unmentioned. Readers of this play may be startled by the presence of a character called "Henry, the Young King" and wonder who is intended. This was actually Henry's son, who was crowned as a kind of junior king in 1170, but died in 1183, before his father.

According to a theory mentioned, but not advocated, by J. Lees, Robin was the son of a Saxon wench whom Henry raised as a companion for Richard and who was Regent of England when Richard was on Crusade. When Richard returned, he outlawed Robin for not coming on Crusade. This highly unlikely scenario is not supported by history.

Henry II is the king at the time of Robin's becoming an outlaw in Peacock's *Maid Marian* (1822) and actually proclaims Robin an outlaw in RHLJ as a result of exaggerated evidence afforded him by the Baron of Nottingham.

HENRY OF LEA In the musical *Arrow* (1995), a knight who, with the Baron of Doncaster, was robbed by Robin and his company. They bore tidings of this to Prince John.

HERB ROBERT A plant known as Robin Hood in Devon.

HERBERT In RHLJ the son of Sir Richard-atte-Lee. In the *Gest*, we are told Sir Richard's son had been under sentence of death for killing a knight in a joust, but in RHLJ he had killed a Norman knight who had abducted his betrothed, the fair Lilas, and for this he had received his sentence.

HEREFORD, BISHOP OF In the ballad BH, this prelate was riding along one day when he and his followers came upon shepherds cooking venison by the roadside. He told them he would arrest them and take them before the King for deerslaying. They pleaded with him, but he would grant them no mercy. Then one of them blew a horn and Robin's followers turned up. The man with the horn was

Robin himself in disguise. The Bishop was taken to Barnsdale where he was made to sup with Robin and his fellowship and he was relieved of £300 in payment. Then Robin caused music to be played and caused the Bishop to dance in his boots before leaving.

HERNE THE HUNTER A person mentioned by Shakespeare who now features in Berkshire legend, but was not associated with Robin until Richard Carpenter penned ROS.

Our first reference to Herne is in Shakespeare's *Merry Wives of Windsor* (? first performed 1597), which tells us that there is an "old tale" that Herne, once a keeper at Windsor Park, walks around a certain oak on winter midnights "with great ragg'd horns", shaking a chain in "a most hideous and dreadful manner", blasting the tree and making the cows yield blood instead of milk. Samuel Ireland, writing in 1792, said Herne was the ghost of a park keeper who had hanged himself. Many think that behind the story lies not a ghost, but the memory of a pagan god. There was a Celtic god called (at least sometimes) Cernunnos, the horned one. M.J. Petry, on the other hand, suggests he was in origin the god Woden. J. Matthews connects his name with Herian, a name sometimes given to Woden (<Old Norse *herjann*, 'lord').

J. Grimm suggested there was a connection between Herne and the Wild Hunt of European folklore. This hunt was supposed to be made up of spectral or supernatural riders who charged through the night. This notion was taken up by W. Harrison Ainsworth in his novel *Windsor Castle* (1843). Herne became the subject of an opera, *Herne, a Legend of Royal Windsor* (1887) by John Old.

Herne has been seen reportedly in local times. It is said he pursues a white deer. In 1976 a soldier guarding the state apartments at Windsor Castle claimed he had seen a statue there grow horns and come to life. Three legends relate to Herne hanging himself, but it must be remembered that Woden, in his Norse form Odin, hanged himself to gain power. One of these tales says that Herne was gored by a stag which he then killed and, madness flooding his brain, he tied the deer's antlers to his head and hanged himself. He is also said to have hanged himself because he was suspected of witchcraft or because Henry VIII had raped his daughter.

In ROS Herne appointed Robin Hood as "Herne's son". His task was to right wrongs, to thwart the oppressors in the land. When the first Robin was killed, he appointed a successor. The Herne of ROS was a man possessed by the god, who lived in a cave behind a waterfall.

Herne, as a result, has become for many a part of the Robin Hood mythos. In the annual Robin Hood festival in Sherwood, Herne the Hunter is one of those who appears. In the stories of the American comic book hero Green Arrow (DC Comics), Robin claimed to be Herne's son.

With the spelling *Hern* he features in Emery's *Tales of Robin Hood* (1988), where he takes the form of a huge stag to battle a magical boar. In this volume he is identified with the Green Man.

HEY DOWN DOWN A DOWN The most popular of the tunes to which the Robin Hood ballads were sung. It was also known as *Arthur-a-Bland, Robin Hood* and *Robin Hood Revived.*

HIDEOUT That the outlaws must have had one or more encampments in the forest goes without saying, though the early ballads do not mention them. In the *Gest*, however, we find Robin had a "lodge" and presumably his followers had similar accommodation, else the rigours of the weather would have been unendurable. In the Sapphire Films *Robin Hood* television series, the hideout included a vegetable patch tended by Little John and from this the outlaws no doubt supplemented their diet of venison. In NARH the outlaws had an entire village in the forest, whose entrance was barred by bushes, which could be drawn back to let people in and out. In fact the outlaws, if really revered by the peasantry, would have required nothing so elaborate, as many goods would have been supplied them by their secret admirers, in the way which often happens with modern day guerrilla fighters. Ritson opines that in the wintertime they probably lived in supporters' houses, or they could have had "tolerably comfortable habitations erected in the woods".

HIGH CELLARER OF ST MARY'S ABBEY In the *Gest* he was held up by Little John and Scarlet (Scarlock). He was brought to Robin's hideout and given a meal, but claimed he had no money to pay for it. He was discovered, upon enquiry, to have £800 upon him, of which he was relieved. Robin's farewell to him ran:

" 'Greet well your abbot,' said Robin
'And your prior too, I pray,
And bid him send me such a monk
                    To dinner every day.' "

HIGH SHERIFF In the *Gest* we are told that the Sheriff of Nottingham went to the High Sheriff to persuade him to rouse the whole country against Robin. The Sheriff had jurisdiction within the city of Nottingham itself, whereas the High Sheriff had jurisdiction over the whole county of Nottinghamshire.

HILARY The name of Robin's innamorata in G.L. Blackwood's *The Lion and the Unicorn* (1982).

HO, JOLLY JENKIN! A song by Sir Arthur Sullivan featured in his opera *Ivanhoe* (1895). The singer was Friar Tuck.

HOB The name given to a kind of sprite in the north of England. Because *Hob* was used as a variant of Robert or Robin, the notion has grown up that Hob may have been an early god from whom Robin descended. Evidence of a kind of cult of Hob is to be found at Hob Hurst's House, a barrow in Derbyshire, where one Hob Thrust was supposed to live. In a cave in Mulgrave Woods (Yorkshire), one Hobthrush Hob was supposed to have dwelt. The term *hob* also denoted a species of sprites and variants of the word include *hobgoblin, hobbin* (in Warwickshire) and *hobyah* (which was found as far north as Scotland and was also imported into New England). The *Denham Tracts* (1895) mention *hobbits,* the only pre-Tolkien mention of such creatures. The Will o' the Wisp was referred to sometimes as *Hob and his Lanthorn* or *Hobby Lantern.* The sprites called *dobies* and *dobbses* are also forms of the name Robin. However, before we infer a Robin-Hood-the-God-Cult derived from these sundry hobs and dobbses, it is worth bearing in mind that the word hob is not found to mean a creature of supernatural kind in any written source before 1450.

HODEKIN A forest sprite in folklore out of which some might argue Robin Hood evolved.

HOOD Persons with this surname are listed under their first names.

HOOD BROOK A stream which flows through the village of Hathersage, where Little John is supposedly buried. It further reinforces the bold outlaw's connections with this area.

HOOK, CAPTAIN Character invented by J.M. Barrie for his play *Peter Pan*. His unexpected presence in this work is because he features in David Hewitt's pantomime *Robin Hood*, having wandered into the wrong production by accident.

HORN, ROBIN HOOD'S A horn, said to have been the outlaw's, mentioned in Redfern's *History of Uttoxeter* (1886). It was exhibited at Loxley Hall in Staffordshire before World War II.

HOUNDS In the Aldine Robin Hood Library pamphlet series, Robin is credited with two hounds, Hector and Vulcan.

HUFFY REDHEART Follower of Robin in the Young Robin Hood series of books by Richard Percy.

HUGO MALAIR A nasty piece of work who carried out Prince John's designs in Joachim Stocqueler's *Maid Marian* (1849).

HUMOUR There have been sundry humorous versions of the Robin Hood story. The *Beano* (UK comic) featured a series called *Robin Hood's Schooldays*. The television series *Maid Marian and her Merry Men* depicts Robin as an upper class idiot, with Marian as the one who really runs the band. Mel Brooks' film *Robin Hood-Men in Tights* also falls into the humorous category, as do sundry Robin Hood pantomimes. A further humorous film treating of this subject is *The Zany Adventures of Robin Hood*. Lionel Bart's stage musical comedy *Twang!!* based on the legend of Robin was not well received and marked the nadir of his career.

HUNTINGDON, EARL OF In several versions of the Robin Hood tale, Robin is the dispossessed Earl of Huntingdon. In *DownfallREH,* we learn that Robin held this title. In Stukeley's *Palaeographica Brittanica* (1743-52), there is an incorrect genealogy stating that Robert Fitzooth, Lord of Kime (Lincolnshire) was also known as Robin Hood and was a pretender to the earldom of Huntingdon. Gutch claims that 'Earl of Huntingdon' was a nickname applied to any hunter. G.P. Kirby in his website *Robin Hood Bold Outlaw of Loxley* suggests that Robin was a Saxon resistance fighter against William I (reigned 1066-87) and that he was the son of Waltheof, last Saxon Earl of Huntingdon, who was beheaded at Winchester in 1076. Loxley Common and Little Haggars Croft formed part of his domain.

In J. Walker McSpadden's *Robin Hood* (1904) and the Disney live action *Robin Hood* (1952), though Robin is not the earl, Marian is the Earl of Huntingdon's daughter.

In the time of Richard I, the actual Earl of Huntingdon was David, brother of William the Lion, King of Scots. After taking Nottingham Castle from Prince John's supporters, king and earl went hunting in Sherwood.

HUNTINGDON FOREST The setting of the adventures in the *Young Robin Hood* television series from the Hanna-Barbera Studios which appeared in 1991.

I

IKA A Japanese martial arts master and assassin who was hired to kill Robin in NARH.

INGLEWOOD A Cumbrian forest which no longer exists. Andrew of Wyntoun maintains Robin Hood operated there. Dobson and Taylor have suggested that

Andrew was confusing Robin with another outlaw, Adam Bell. J. Lees opines that Andrew means 'English Wood' and is in fact referring to Sherwood. However, it is not impossible that Robin was associated with this part of the country. A fragment of poetry has been discovered mentioning Robin Hood and "keen men of cumber". The last word here may stand for Cumberland, the former county (now part of Cumbria) in which Inglewood once stood.

INGRID A sister of Little John in NARH.

IVANHOE The hero of the novel *Ivanhoe* (1818) by Sir Walter Scott. His full name was Sir Wilfrid of Ivanhoe. Much of the novel features him in a castle which is besieged by his father's serfs and Robin and his band. The Black Knight (King Richard in disguise) and Friar Tuck also figure largely in the story. A tongue-in-cheek sequel to *Ivanhoe* is to be found in W.M. Thackeray's *Rowena and Rebecca* (1843). Many readers of the original work felt that Ivanhoe should have married the vivacious Rebecca rather than the nondescript Rowena. In this work Rowena, thinking Ivanhoe dead, married Athelstane. It must have been a shock when Ivanhoe returned, but she was on her deathbed anyway, which saved everyone a lot of trouble and enabled Ivanhoe to wed Rebecca, now turned Christian. Marriage to her while she was Jewish would have been socially unthinkable in the Middle Ages. Robin, Marian and Friar Tuck all appear in the story.

J

JACK The Potter's boy in the 16th Century play *Robin Hood and the Potter*. He became considerably distressed when Robin broke the Potter's pots. The play does not survive in complete form, or so it is generally supposed..

JACK IN THE GREEN The figure of a boy dressed in greenery who appeared in processions of chimney sweeps. Some have held Jack to be a fertility spirit and identical with Robin Hood. There are some objections to this, however. R. Judge has shown that chimney sweeps were unknown before the 18th Century. The earliest reference to Jack is possibly in J. Strutt's *Sports and Pastimes of the People of England* (1801). This would seem to indicate that Jack was invented in fairly modern times, unless the sweepers of soot took him from some earlier folklore source. An article by J. Minfie in *English Dance and Song*, Spring, 1978, states that in Whitstable (Kent), Robin and Marian formed part of Jack's entourage, which would indicate that there Robin and Jack were quite separate characters.

JAMES III, King of Scotland (reigned 1460-88). Because the play *George-a-Green* (1599) was set in the reign of Edward IV, he was the King of Scotland at the time. In the play, he had invaded England, but had been defeated. Robin and George encountered him and Edward, when both kings were in disguise.

JARNSAXA In NARH an Irish giant who aided Robin by helping him defeat the evil Ferris, whom he had previously cured with his magic breath.. Jarnsaxa was the last of the Femorians. The name *Jarnsaxa* was originally that of a giantess in Norse mythology, who was supposed to have had a son by Thor. The word 'Femorians' is a corruption of Fomorians (Irish *Fomhoraigh*) which was the name of a monstrous race in Irish mythology.

JEM OF NETHERBEE In LS, an outlaw whose band was joined by some of Robin's men after his death.

JEMIMA A prostitute who joins Robin in Clayton Emery's forthcoming book *Little John and the Bells of London.*

JENKIN A sharp-witted servant of George-a-Green, in the anonymous play about that worthy.

JENNET In ROS an herbalist whom the Sheriff tried to force to use her knowledge of magic to capture Robin. The brew she devised left the outlaws senseless, but Marian, shown a vision by Herne, made them regurgitate their meal, so they were ready when the Sheriff's soldiers turned up.

JENNY Marian's maid in Noyes' *Robin Hood.*

JINNY The name of Will Scarlet's sister in *DownfallREH.* She went into Sherwood disguised as a boy to join her brother and Robin, accompanied by Friar Tuck. There seems to have been an independent tradition, no longer recorded, that the Friar fell in love with Jinny and for some reason tumbled into a well. There is a ballad found in Child (no. 276) which deals with a girl who tricks a friar into falling into a well, but in this neither is named.

JOAN The name of Robin's mother in BBVM.

JOHN, PRINCE Younger brother of Richard I, born 1167, died 1217. In 1189 he married Isabella, daughter of the Earl of Gloucester. The marriage was childless. In 1200 he married Isabelle, daughter of the Count of Angouleme. Their children were Richard, Henry, Joan, Isabella and Eleanor. He became King of England in 1199. His most famous act as king was the signing of Magna Carta in 1215.

During Richard's absence on Crusade, John had garrisoned many castles with his own men and he actually took Nottingham Castle by force. On Richard's return, most of the castles capitulated to him, but he had to attack Nottingham. When he seized it, John was tried and banished, but soon pardoned.

Tales placing Robin in the reign of Richard I make Prince John a powerful enemy of the outlaw, while Robin is cast as a resistance leader, loyal to Richard. In *DownfallREH*, John's opposition to Robin was because he was in love with Marian. In this play John's character is somewhat ambivalent, as it was intended for an Elizabethan audience and John, though unpopular in his own day, was quite admired by the Elizabethans. ROS continues Robin's activities into John's reign.

John, incidentally, was the first monarch styled *King of England;* his predecessors had used the title *King of the English.*

JOHN BULL ROBIN The hero's name in a Gloucestershire mummers' play. The "John Bull" element of the name is easily explained – it was that of the typical Englishman. The "Robin" element quite possibly comes from Robin Hood.

JOHN ROWYE A character in a Robin Hood play at Anthony (Cornwall). He appears to be Little John, provided with a surname not generally known.

K

KARIN Robin's innamorata in the film *Robin Hood i Pirati* (1960).

KAROLIN The brother of Earine in Jonson's *Sad Shepherd.* He fell in love with Amie.

KATE An attendant of Marian in Tennyson's *The Foresters.*

KATHERINE, QUEEN She features on two ballads. The first, QK, tells how she sent for Robin and his men to shoot in her behalf against the King's archers at Finsbury Park. After the contest, Katherine asked that her bowmen be unmolested and then revealed they were Robin and his followers. In RHC the King, here named Henry, pursued Robin after he had left the court but could not catch up with him. Robin doubled back and visited the Queen while the King was in the north. When the King came back, he was furious that Robin had been at court in his absence.

There seems no doubt that the king here is Henry VIII (reigned 1509-1547), but he would be much too late for an historical Robin. The ballads seem to be based on the fact that Henry probably held contests where persons dressed up as Robin and his band participated. In this case we may ask who was Queen Katherine, as Henry had three queens of that name. Katherine of Aragon has been suggested and indeed we learn that in a Maying ceremony in 1515, she and Henry watched 'Robin Hood' and archers shooting. J. Bellamy, an historian whose views are always worth listening to, however, favours Katherine Howard.

KATHERINE DE MORTRAIN Robin's cousin in Sharon Drake's *Damsel in Distress*
(1992), where she was pursued by Damian Mountjoy, her guardian.

KEMAL A notable Saracen ally of Robin in NARH. He was betrothed to a princess named Kadija.

KENDAL GREEN While Robin and his followers are usually thought of as wearing Lincoln Green, they are sometimes depicted as being dressed in Kendal Green.

This was cloth of a bottle-green shade, made by Flemish weavers.

KENNETH A brother of Marian needing rescue from Prince John in J.R. Crawford's play *Robin of Sherwood* (1912).

KET AND HOB Two small persons mistaken for fairies because of their height in Henry Gilbert's *Robin Hood* (1913).

KIME Stukeley claimed that the real Robin Hood was Ralph Fitzooth, a member of the family who ruled this village in Lincolnshire. However, Stukeley's pedigree will not withstand historical investigation.

KING Many people assume the king in Robin's time was Richard the Lionheart, as he features as such in many books and films. However, there is disagreement amongst the sources. The *Gest* calls him 'Edward our comely king' but does not say which Edward is intended; *see* **Edward II**. In that source he went into the forest disguised as a monk. Robin invited him to dinner. There was an archery contest. Whoever failed to hit a garland with an arrow was to receive a buffet from Robin. Eventually, Robin missed and received a buffet from the King which laid him on the ground. Robin divined he was no monk and, realising his identity, craved pardon for himself and his men. The King invited him to court. He was later allowed to return to a chapel he claimed to have founded, but, although given only a week's leave, never came back to London. Edward II actually made a progress in the north between April and November 1323, so he is generally identified with the Edward of the *Gest*. In RHM reference is made to "our comely king" without naming him. John Major, a Scottish historian, is the first to place Robin in the reign of Richard

I. He is also mentioned as the king concerned in Parker, KD and GA. Edward IV and a King Henry, who is clearly meant to be Henry VIII, are also mentioned, but they would be much too late for an historical Robin Hood; *see* **Edward IV** and **Katherine, Queen.**

KING JOHN'S PALACE A hunting lodge, the remains of which are yet to be seen behind the Dog and Duck Inn in the Nottinghamshire village of Old Clipstone. According to legend, some hostages were kept there and Robin Hood mounted an attack from Cresswell Crags to set them free.

KINGHAM Also known as the King-Game, this was enacted in days of yore at Kingston-upon-Thames (Surrey). Robin Hood was combined with a hobby horse in this event, which also featured Maid Marian and Friar Tuck. A commemorative window depicting this event is to be seen in Kingston Museum. It was designed by a Dr Finny in 1911.

KIRKLEES A priory of Dominican nuns where, according to many sources, Robin met his death. The priory was dissolved in 1538 and Kirklees House now stands on its former site at Hatshead (Yorkshire).

Feeling ill and now well stricken in years, Robin set off for Kirklees with Little John to be bled by his cousin, the prioress. She is sometimes identified with an Elizabeth de Stainton. In the ballad *Robin Hood His Death* , he was cursed on the way by an old woman. As part of the ballad is missing here, we cannot tell what this was all about. He also encountered women weeping for him. All this is very mysterious and has an eerie ritualistic air to it. Again, owing to the ballad's fragmentary state, we do not know who these women were. The ballad then tells us that Robin gave the Prioress £20 for the bleeding. She started the bleeding, but then abandoned him in a chamber, leaving him to bleed to death. Into the chamber, to make sure he would rise no more, came Red Roger, who stabbed him in the side with his sword, whereupon Robin, still with some strength left, clove him between head and shoulders, killing him. Little John wanted to burn the priory, but Robin, who would never harm women, forbade him. He told John to carry him to "yonder street" and there to make him a fair grave of gravel and grit.

In the *Gest* Red Roger is called Sir Roger of Doncaster.

The ballad *Robin Hood's Death and Burial* is less fragmentary. In this, the dying Robin summoned Little John with his horn. Robin urged John to hand him his bow and let him fire an arrow. Wheresoever it landed, there he was to be interred.

In Sebastian Evans' *Of Robin Hood's Death and Burial* (1865), Robin's sister was the Abbess of Kirklees, where he was staying in sanctuary, but she played no part in his death, which was caused by Lord Perryn and Lord Newbay.

KIRKLEES, PRIORESS OF The Prioress of Kirklees is unnamed in ballad history, but guesses have been made as to her identity. One candidate was Elizabeth de Stainton, whose gravestone was discovered in 1706 in what is called the Nun's Grave. The dates of Elizabeth's office are uncertain, perhaps 1331-47. However W.R. Mitchell says that a document owned by a local family avers that Joanna de Stainton, known in religion as Sister Ursula, took in a sick and aged outlaw called Robert de Locksley in 1248.

KIT O' THIRSK In the ballad *Robin Hood and the Pedlars*, he was one of the pedlars concerned and knocked Robin out, but revived him with a balsam.

KITE In Emery's *Tales of Robin Hood* (1988) the evil huntsman of Guy of Gisborne. He sacrificed a baby as part of a magical rite to unleash the baneful magic boar into the forest. Eventually, he was killed by Hern (*sic*) the Hunter in stag form.

L

LAMBIE   This was the name of a senior officer of the Baron of Nottingham in RHLJ. He was the commander of the troops who killed Robin's foster-mother, Margaret Hood, and Robin slew him with an arrow.

LANCE   The loyal hound of Gilbert Hood in RHLJ. He threw himself into his master's grave.

LAND AND FELIX   Two evil barons in *The Rock'n'Roll Robin Hood* (music David Wall, Don Hillan and Dale Alison; libretto Don Hillan).

LEA, MARGARET   In Michael Cadnum's *Forbidden Forest* (2002), she was fated to wed Sir Gilbert, who was fortunately stabbed before this event could occur. Everyone thought Margaret had done it, so she went to the forest to join Robin.

LINCOLN   The retainer of Gilbert Hood in RHLJ. He later joined Robin's band.

LINCOLN GREEN   The colour of clothing generally thought to have been worn by Robin and his men for camouflage purposes. This colour was applied to cloth by first dyeing it blue with woad, which had long been cultivated in Lincolnshire, and then overdyeing it with yellow, obtained from weld or dyer's greenweed. Lincoln was supposed, according to Michael Drayton (1563-1631), to have the best green dyed cloth in England. Rather more expensive was Lincoln scarlet, while Lincoln grey was cheaper. All these varieties of cloth were produced by Lincoln's three textile crafts guilds.

LISBETH Daughter of Lord Brooks in the Italian film *Robin Hood i Pirati* (1960). She fell in love with Robin, who did not reciprocate her sentiments.

LITTLE DUNMOW The Lady Chapel of the Priory Church of Little Dunmow (Essex) contains a tomb reputed to be that of Maid Marian. The actual effigy on the tomb is that of Joan Devereux (died 1409), mother of Walter FitzWalter (died 1431).

LITTLE HAGGAR'S CROFT Writing in 1637, J. Harrison said that in Little Haggar's Croft lay the foundation of the house or cottage where Robin Hood was born. A wooded area, Loxley Firth, surrounded it. There is a belief that the present Normandale House (Yorkshire) was built on the site of Little Haggar's Croft.

LITTLE JOHN He was Robin Hood's henchman, mentioned by balladeer and chronicler alike. His name was said to have been originally John Little, but was changed for jocose reasons into Little John by Will Stutely, because of his height. However, Ritson, citing no source, avers that his surname was Naylor. A post-Ritsonian tradition has him living in Mansfield with his father, George Naylor. A local tradition recorded by J. Lees says that his name was originally John of the Little Wood.

In the Robin Hood mythos he is depicted as a mighty fighter equipped with a quarterstaff, but also as intelligent and sensible. The suggestion that he had a saga of his own and was only latterly linked with Robin Hood has little to support it.

Robin's meeting with him occurs in the ballad *Robin Hood and Little John.* Robin and he encountered each other on a bridge when Robin was about twenty (in another version collected in Virginia, fifteen) and neither would give way to the other. Robin was at first inclined to use his bow, but, being taunted by John as a coward because he had "naught but a staff", he cut a staff for himself and, so armed, took on his gigantic adversary. Robin did not fare well: he ended up in the water. Emerging, he winded his horn. His band arrived and, seeing their sopping commander, were minded to fling John into the river, but Robin bade them forbear. John joined the band and Stutely "christened" him with his new name. This fight is supposed to have taken place on the River Went (Yorkshire) or on Coxley Beck near Wakefield.

In the *Gest*, Little John, using the nom de guerre of Reynold Greenleaf, entered the service of the Sheriff of Nottingham. One day, during the Sheriff's absence, he tried to take food from the kitchen, much to the chagrin of the cook. The two fought and then made peace, the cook agreeing to join Robin's band. He and John quitted Nottingham Castle, taking with them £300 and silver plate. In the forest John (still posing as Reynold) lured the Sheriff into Robin's clutches, where he was forced to take an oath not to bother the outlaws any more. (They actually believed the Sheriff would honour this oath – obviously they did not know him for the scallywag he truly was). Later in the work, when Robin's band were forced to flee Nottingham after the Sheriff's archery contest, John was wounded in the knee, but Much the Miller's Son carried him to safety on his back.

The ballad *Robin Hood and Guy of Gisborne* makes John the killer of the Sheriff.

John is the hero of a ballad of his own, *Little John Goes a-Begging.* Here he encountered and trounced three fraudulent beggars, who were pretending to be disabled and were nothing like so poor as they seemed and relieved them of a large sum of money.

Little John was with Robin at the last. After the Prioress of Kirklees had killed Robin by bleeding him, John carried him to the place her had indicated for burial.

Subsequently Little John is said to have gone to Ireland, where he made an astonishing shot from a bridge over the River Liffey in Dublin. One tradition claims he was executed for theft at Arbour Hill in that city. However, Holinshed's *Chronicle,* of which Shakespeare made much use, claims he left Ireland and went to Moray in Scotland. There, according to Scottish historian Hector Boece (died 1536), he died and was buried at Pette. Elsewhere it is said he retired to Hathersage (Derbyshire), his place of birth, where he at length died. What was allegedly his cottage was pulled down not long ago. His traditional grave is still to be seen in the churchyard there. In 1929 the Ancient Order of Foresters marked it with two stones and agreed to care for it. When the grave was opened in the 18th Century, several large bones were found. One, a 29.5" thighbone was removed and subsequently stolen. What was claimed to be his bow, 79" long, tipped with horn and made of spliced yew, was hanging in the parish church until 1729, together with some armour, also reputedly the outlaw's. The bow was taken to Cannon Hall because of the run-down state of the church. It was eventually inherited by one Simon Frazer and was in his possession in Scotland in 1980. Other traditions have John buried at Thorpe Salvin near Worksop and Wincle (Cheshire).

On the Longshaw estate near Hathersage Little John's Well is to be found. Another exists adjoining the Doncaster-Wakefield Road in Yorkshire. There is a hill in Charnwood Forest near Leicester which is called simply Little John, while Little John's Stone is to be found in Leicester itself. There is a tradition that Robin Hood and Little John met for the last time at the Robin Hood and

Little John Inn in Castleton (Yorkshire). The present building dates only from 1671, but it is not impossible it stands on the site of some older structure.

Various personages have been suggested as the original of Little John. If we accept that he and Robin flourished in the reign of Edward II, we find a number of records relating to persons bearing his name. One held the somewhat unlikely post of a sea-captain in the royal service at various times between 1332 and 1335. Another (or perhaps even the same one operating on land) was accused of breaking into the park of the Archbishop of York and carrying off deer. Interestingly, one of his companions bore the name Robert. James Myers in *Derbyshire Rambles* (1924) argues that we might identify him with a Jack Crawney, who owned property in Hathersage in 1352. Perhaps, suggests Myers, he might even have written the *Gest* itself, as he was credited with the composition of poems. It would certainly be astonishing if Little John proved to be the author of the major Robin Hood work of balladry.

Little John is the hero of a recent novel *Forbidden Forest* (2002) by Michael Cadnum. In this we are told John's surname was Tannerson, he was a ferryman outlawed as a result of an accidental killing and was enamoured of Margaret Lea. In the musical *Arrow* (1995), Little John was the original leader of the outlaw band, who handed over command to Robin.

LOCKSLEY (also **LOXLEY**) The place often associated with Robin Hood. In garlands of Robin Hood poems, Robin is sometimes referred to as Sir Robert of Loxley. According to BBVM it lay in Nottinghamshire. Another tradition places it in Staffordshire, where there is a village of this name. Here Robin was supposed to have spent his honeymoon with Clorinda the shepherdess and a Robin Hood's Horn was kept here in days gone by. The Sloane *Life of Robin Hood* says it was in Yorkshire and there is a hamlet of this name near Sheffield. Outside this village was Loxley Chase containing a cottage called Little Haggar's Croft which John Harrison in 1637 thought to be Robin's birthplace.

J.R. Planche thought the Locksley of Robin was Loxley in Warwickshire. He claimed the Fitzooth family whom Stukeley had erroneously claimed were Lords of Kime , were it fact the FitzOdos, Lords of Loxley (Warwickshire). He would identify Robin Hood with Robert FitzOdo who inherited his title of Lord of Loxley Manor in the reign of Henry II (1154-89) and there he ruled until 1196. He may then have died, but it is also possible he was disinherited for a number of records mention a Robert Fitz Odo, perhaps the same person, as being alive somewhat later. If he had lost title and inheritance, this would have happened in the reign of Richard I. In 1196, Loxley Manor had fallen to Peter de Mora, who was married to Robert's daughter, Basilia.

LOCKSLEY, WILLIAM An obscure follower of Robin mentioned in VK. In RHGP there is a character named Loxley who seems distinct from Robin Hood.

LONDON The metropolis seems to lack any direct association with Robin Hood, but it has over the years boasted various Robin Hood place names.. There were formerly no less than five Robin Hood Courts, all of which have now disappeared. A Robin Hood Lane has existed from at least 1703, when it is referred to as "Robin Hood's Lane", while a Robin Hood Yard lies north of Holborn. The London May Games of 1559 featured Robin Hood, Little John, Marian and Friar Tuck. Anthony Munday wrote a pageant for the Lord Mayor's Day in 1615. In this he made Marian the daughter of the first lord mayor of that city, who lived in the reign of Richard I.

LOXLEY *see* **Locksley.**

LUDLOW CHURCH There is an iron arrow in the roof of this Shropshire church. While its original purpose was to mark the meeting place of the Ludlow fletchers, a tradition has grown up that it was shot by Robin Hood. He had been aiming for the weathercock, but this was not one of his more successful shots.

LYNDRIC A hill near Dale Abbey described in the ballad *Robin Whood Turned Hermit* (1735) by Francis Peck as 'famous'. Here Robin had a strange dream which persuaded him to take up the eremitical life.

M

MAERIN The name given to Marian in Reyne Thera Lorele's *The Archer King* (1999). This makes her the daughter of Ranulf fitz Warin, Baron of Derby.

MAID MARIAN *see* **Marian.**

MAID MARIAN'S BOW A lady's bow that was shown as Thoresby Hall in Nottinghamshire. A tradition grew up that it had been Maid Marian's.

MAJOR OAK An oak tree in Sherwood Forest. This was supposed to be the site of Robin's headquarters. In its hollow, it was averred, Robin and his men would hide from pursuers. It still exists, having narrowly missed being blown up in World War II. Some claim the tree is 800 years old, which would make it far too young to have been Robin's hideaway. Some, however, would argue that it is far older , dating from about 500 AD. It has, at various times, been called the Queen's Oak and the Cockpen or

Cockpit Tree. It takes its present name from a Major Hayman Rook.

Latterly, it had been sustained by iron chains and braces, but these have now been replaced by a less obtrusive steel system.

In J.O. Smith's pantomime *Robin Hood* (1990), Major Oak was the name of the captain of the Sheriff's guard.

MALINCHE, LA Also known as Marina, she features in Mexican dances and M. Harris has suggested she and Marian (as a dancer in the May Games) share a common origin.

MARCEL OAKSTAFF A follower of Robin in the Young Robin Hood series by Richard Percy.

MARGARET HOOD Robin's adoptive mother in RHLJ. She was the sister of Roland Ritson, a man steeped in villainy. She was eventually killed when her house was attacked by the forces of the Baron of Nottingham.

MARIAN (also **MARION**) A medieval diminutive of Mary, used for Robin's innamorata. For purposes of consistency, the spelling *Marian* will be used throughout.

In the ballad MM (17th Century), Marian had been in love with Robin since before his outlawry. She dressed as a page and went into the woods, seeking him. Neither recognised the other when they met, as both were in disguise. They had a fight and Marian proved no pushover when it came to swordplay. Each wounded the other. Robin asked her to join his band because of her valour and then discovered her identity.

As will be seen from the date of this ballad, Marian seems a latecomer to the Robin Hood saga. The French *pastourelles* featured a couple called Robin and Marion and these may have been incorporated into the May Games,

Robin then being identified with Robin Hood. The first actual mention of Maid Marian seems to have been in Alexander Barclay's *Ship of Fools* (1500).

In *DownfallREH* we are told that Marian's real name was Matilda, daughter of Lord Fitzwater. He seems to have brought in here another character, unconnected originally with Marian, who was beloved by Prince John according to story.   One version of this tale is found in Weever's *Ancient Funeral Monuments* (1631): King John desired Matilda, daughter of Lord Fitzwalter, but both father and daughter spurned him, so he poisoned Matilda. An earlier version of the tale is to be found in Drayton's *Matilda the Fair* (1594). Thus Munday made John pursue Matilda, who took to the woods and became Maid Marian.

Marian is shown in the ballad to be no mean warrior. In both ROS and NARH this tradition is maintained. In the latter series she is called a 'lady warrior' and, one suspects, is modelled on Xena Warrior Princess. For some reason Charles Gilson's *Robin of Sherwood* (1960) makes her Robin's sister, loved by Alan-a-Dale, while in Edith Hail's *Robin Hood* (1928) she was enamoured of Will Scarlet. In some retellings she fled to Sherwood to avoid the embraces of an unwanted suitor, for example, in Rosemary Sutcliffe's *Chronicles of Robin Hood* (1950), she was evading the attentions of Roger of Doncaster, in E. Charles Vivian's *Robin Hood* (1927), Robin rescued her from a forced marriage to Baron de Beleme, while in Antonia Frazer's *Robin Hood* (1955), Oswald Montdragon was putting in an unwanted appearance on her marital horizon.

In Peacock's *Maid Marian* (1822), she was the daughter of Lord Arlingford, while Jennifer Roberson's *Lady of the Forest* styles her Lady Marian of Ravenskeep. She was the daughter of Sir Richard atte Lee (in various forms of his name) in Tennyson's *Foresters* and ROS, the daughter of the Earl of Whitby according to Antonia Frazer and that of the Earl of Huntingdon in the Disney live action version of

Robin Hood. Death REH calls her the daughter of Lord Fitzwater, a name taken from the Matilda story; but she has tended to be given the surname Fitzwater and Fitzwalter as a result. In this play Munday contradicts himself by calling her the daughter of Lord Lacey.

The most bizarre conclusion to the story of Robin and Marian is to be found in the film *Robin and Marian* (1976). Here she became the Prioress of Kirklees who poisoned Robin, so he would avoid the burdens of old age and outlawry. For good measure, she poisoned herself.

A late legend says that, after Robin's death, Marian lived in Dunmow Priory in Essex, whither King John sent her a poisoned bracelet by the unwitting Robert de Medewe. The latter actually fell in love with her and, after delivering the envenomed wristband, turned and came back to find her dead. Heartbroken, he threw himself on her bier.

Few placenames seem to be called after Marian, though there is a Maid Marian Way, a modern name, in contemporary Nottingham.

MARINA A friend of Matilda in the anonymous work *Robin Hood an Opera* (1730). The librettist here seems to have re-split Marian and Matilda into two characters. Marina was in love with Little John.

MARION *see* **Marian.**

MARK, PHILIP An historical character. In Richard Kluger's novel *Sheriff of Nottingham* (1993), Philip Mark was a good man, intent on stamping out official corruption. With this end in view he did a deal with Robin Hood.

The historical Philip Mark, who was Sheriff of Nottinghamshire and Derbyshire 1209-24 and custodian of Sherwood Forest 1212-17, is not reflected in this character.

An episode in ROS has him become Sheriff of Nottingham and here he is referred to as 'the Butcher of Lincoln'.

MARTHA She became the wife of Will Scarlet in MacNally's opera *Robin Hood* (1784). He had been in love with Stella, but she had been denied him because of his treacherous behaviour.

MARX, GROUCHO Due to an outrageous anachronism, this well-known bespectacled and moustachioed comedian is a member of Robin's band in the humorous *Robin Hood According to Spike Milligan* (1999).

MARY Name of both Arthur-a-Bland's wife and daughter in Emery's *Tales of Robin Hood* (1988).

MASKED MARVEL In DC Comics *Robin Hood Tales* # 12, we encounter an archer supposedly superior to Robin, but our suspicions should naturally be aroused by his wearing a mask. The Masked Marvel proved to be Robin Hood himself and the 'Robin Hood' he outshot was Will Scarlet doing an impersonation.

MATTHEW In ROS the father of Much He was a miller who had been Robin's foster father. He lost his life at hand of Guy of Gisborne.

MAUDE In RHLJ, the maidservant of Christabel, much given to osculation. She originally fell in love with Robin, but, her passion being unrequited, became enamoured of Will Scarlet, whom she eventually married.

MAUDLIN The witch of Papplewick (located in Sherwood) in Ben Jonson's unfinished play, *The Sad Shepherd.* She captured Earine, the beloved of Aeglamour, and imprisoned her in a tree, intending her for her son,

Lorel. When Robin was holding a feast she turned up in the likeness of Maid Marian. In this guise, she sent the venison to herself (in her real persona as a witch) and had a remarkable quarrel with Robin. She also had a daughter named Douce, to whom she gave Earine's clothes to enhance her attractiveness. Robin suspected that the woman he was dealing with was Maudlin disguised as Marian, so he pulled off her girdle, as a result of which her spell was broken and her true shape revealed.

MAXFIELD The ballad PA tells us Will Scarlet's father was the son of the Earl of Maxfield, but where Maxfield was is uncertain. It may have been Maxfield Plain (Yorkshire) or even Macclesfield.

MAY, LADY The month of May personified, she was sometimes part of Robin's company in the May Games.

MAY GAMES Games held traditionally in the Spring to celebrate the departure of Winter. They took place sometimes, but not always, on 1st May. The term 'maying' was applied to them.

Robin Hood found his way into the May Games and not just in the north of England, his familiar stamping ground. The May Games were probably influenced by the French *pastourelles*, which featured characters called Robin and Marion, Robin being identified by the Englishry as Robin Hood. One of these, *Le Jeu de Robin and Marion* by Adam de la Halle was translated into English by John Gower about 1377. This may well be how Maid Marian entered the Robin Hood mythos. Robin seems to have taken the place of the May King and may have ousted a character called the Abbot of Unreason, who had occupied that place hitherto. However, Robin was far from featuring in all May Games:: of 104 locations of May Games noted between 1450 and 1550, Robin appears only in twenty-four. He is styled King of the May in Scotland in 1577. Lewis Spence argued that he was a May King who reigned from one year to the next, but here he drifted into unsubstantiated speculation.

MERION A son of Robin Hood in Paul A. Castleton's *Son of Robin Hood* (1941). He joined his father in the greenwood.

MERLIN The magician associated with King Arthur (in Welsh *Myrddin*). In NARH, he was the teacher of the wizard Olwyn. In Gary Yershon's *Robin Hood* (1966), he had been imprisoned in an oak tree, but was eventually released.

MILES DE FALCONET A knight affianced to Marian in the film *Robin Hood* (1991).
Marian was not amenable to marrying him, so she made her escape into the wildwood.

MONEY The currency in Robin Hood's time was the system which obtained in England before decimalisation, i.e., twelve pence (abbreviation d. from Latin *denarii*)=one shilling (abbreviation s. from Latin *solidus* plural *solidi*); twenty shillings=one pound (£). However, a number of denominations are mentioned in the Robin Hood stories which require explanation. A *noble* was equal to 6s./8d. (1/3£); an *angel* was equal to 10s./0d. (1/2£) and a *mark* was 13s./4d. (2/3£). The term *groat* was used to mean four pence (4d.).

MONK This anonymous cleric features in the ballad RHM. Robin had despoiled him of £100, which had rankled greatly with him. Seeing Robin at church in Nottingham, he told the Sheriff and Robin was arrested. The Monk was then sent to the King for instructions, but was waylaid on the road by Little John, who killed him. With his letter, John and Much went to the King, who gave them his royal seal, with instructions to bring Robin back to him. With this seal they gained audience with the Sheriff, who bade them stay overnight. They told the Sheriff that the Monk whom he had sent had been promoted to the dizzying height of Abbot of Westminster. During the night they rescued Robin and brought him back to the greenwood.

MOODY, TOM In Robin McKinley's *Outlaws of Sherwood* (1988), he engaged Robin in an archery contest. Robin won and Tom tried to kill him. Robin shot an arrow at Tom's right leg, but missed and killed him, thereby occasioning his outlawry.

MOOT HALL This building in Nottingham had dungeons underneath it and J. Lees argues it his here that Robin would have been imprisoned during the action of RHM.

MORRIS DANCE A traditional English dance, perhaps introduced from overseas at a comparatively late date. Elizabethan practice led to its being confused with the May Games. The original name of this terpsichorean entertainment is said to have been 'Moorish dance' and one of the characters had a blackened face and was called Murrian (Moorish one), perhaps the origin of Marian. J. Brand argues that the word Murrian was derived from Italian *morione*, 'head piece'. Robin Hood, Marian and Friar Tuck were all in time featured in the Morris Dance. While today Morris dancers wear white, of yore they were clad in green, like Robin Hood's men.

MORTIANA A witch in NARH. She worked for Prince John, who traded a year of his life for her to bring back the soldiers of Alexander the Great to use against Robin. She did, but they failed to defeat the outlaws.

MUCH, THE MILLER'S SON An important member of Robin's band, he is sometimes called *Midge* and on one occasion *Nick*. Legend has it that he was born in Wakefield. Forest officials captured him and his hound hunting and said they would cut off the hound's forepaws. Much rescued the unhappy beast, aided by Little John and Will Scarlet and joined Robin's band.

Although in the *Gest* he is referred to as 'little Much', he seems to have been a strapping character. The *Gest* tells us there was not an inch of Much's body that was not the equal of a whole man. He carried Little John to safety on his back when the latter was wounded. He must obviously have been thought of as possessing considerable strength.

The mill his father worked was said to have been the King's Mill on the River Calder, demolished in 1932; but there is a ballad called *The King and the Miller* involving the Miller of Mansfield, whom some have identified with Much. Another tradition makes him the son of the Miller of Wakefield. J. Lees argues that Much was possibly the son of the miller of Bobbers Mill, near Nottingham.

In ROS, Robin was adopted by Much's father and he and Much grew up as brothers. In this series Much is represented as being a little simple-minded. In Clayton Emery's *Tales of Robin Hood* (1988), he is depicted as being actually retarded. In RHLJ we are told that his real name was Midge and Much but a nickname, while his surname was Cockle, but he did not care to use it.

When Much entered the May Games, he was a sort of jester who, with an inflated bladder, would run about striking the heads of onlookers.

MUMMING Mummers went around country villages, usually at Christmas, and existed in the Middle Ages.

However, a particular form of entertainment called the Mummers' Play is what concerns us here, particularly a type of such play called the Combat Play. In this, the Mummers would enter each house in the village as part of the season's festivities. Originally they were clad in strips of paper, but later the costume could be more elaborate. A presenter - often Father Christmas, a rather wilder character than the Santa Claus of today - would ask for room and a small and sometimes woodenly performed playlet was acted out. This usually involved two fighters – often St George and a Turkish knight, the latter perhaps originally intended as a dragon substitute.. St George would be killed and a doctor would revive him. In some versions of the play Robin Hood would be a combatant and material from the ballads incorporated. In the Shipton-Under-Wychwood mummers' play, Robin is the hero, Little John is killed and he is revived by Dr Good. A modern such play is *The Robin Hood Mummers Play*
by Philip Scotese. This was written for the Guild of St Ives at the Bristol Renaissance Faire.

As to the origin of the plays, they have all the hallmarks of a midwinter fertility play, showing winter is on the way out and the new year of leaf and growth is being revived, as signified by the Doctor reviving the corpse. Unfortunately, there are problems with such an interpretation. These plays themselves are not mentioned by any antiquarian before the 18th Century, which would surely have been a great oversight on their part. No texts antedating this time have been found. If they were genuine rustic fertility rituals dating from pagan times, one would expect them to be in dialect, but they are couched in standard English. One can only surmise that the idea of the mummers' play was concocted by some educated person in the 1700s and spread widely about the country.

MURDACH, ROBERT The name of the Sheriff of Nottingham in Henry Gilbert's *Robin Hood and his Merry Men* (1914). It was also used in the American ME Comics *Robin Hood* series. In fact, a Ralph Murdach was the actual name of the Sheriff in the first year of Richard I.

N

NASIR A very popular character in the series ROS; in fact, he came to have his own fan club. His full name was Nasir Malek Khemal Inal Ibrahim Shams ad Duala Walthab ibn Mahmud. He was a Saracen who, perhaps under duress, served the evil Simon de Belleme, but subsequently joined Robin's band. He was a somewhat enigmatic character, silent of aspect, who ate apart from the others.

NATALIE A sister of Little John in NARH. Delouche, a man with magical armour, rounded her up for a beauty contest to be held before Prince John. First prize was Delouche, while all other contestants faced execution. Robin had to rescue her, but he required a golden arrow, property of Prince John, to do this.

NEEDWOOD A royal forest in Staffordshire. Legend had it that Robin Hood hunted deer here and robbed passers-by on the nearby highway. A stone in the forest marks the place where Robin hid to escape the King. On the edge of the forest was a house said to have been built on the site of the house where Robin was born.

NEWARK, EARL OF The villain in the film *Sword of Sherwood Forest* (1960). He planned to murder the Regent of England, but was thwarted by Robin.

NORMANS The inhabitants of Normandy, descended from Vikings who had set up a state there. In 1066 William II, Duke of Normandy, invaded England and conquered it, becoming King William I. This meant that the ruling population of England was largely Norman, speaking Norman French, while the bulk of the populace spoke Old English, or Anglo-Saxon as Cantabrigians prefer to call it. The native inhabitants were termed Saxons (hence Modern Irish, Scottish Gaelic *Sasanach*, Scots *Sassenach,* Welsh *Sais,* an Englishman). The racial differences between rulers and ruled are often emphasised in retellings of the Robin Hood tales, but whether they persisted long enough to influence the original stories is hard to determine.

NOTTINGHAM The medieval city lay just south of Sherwood Forest and the Sheriff was ever the bane of Robin and vice-versa. It originally grew up around the homestead of a man named Snot, but at some stage the initial letter was dropped, else today it would be called Snottingham. Estimates for the medieval population of the town vary from 3000-5000 (13th Century). The town walls were to the north and west of the city, with ditches to the east. The Saxon element of the population lived in the south-east and here St Mary's Church, where Robin was betrayed by the Monk, was located. Nottingham Castle was in the south-western part. The present Nottingham Castle is a later building. To the south of the city flowed the River Leen. There were four gates in the north wall. It contained an inn which is now called *The Tryppe to Jerusalem.*

When Richard I returned to England in 1194, he had to capture the Castle, which was in the hands of Prince John's men. Banishment was pronounced on Prince John in the great hall of the castle.

In front of the Castle, on Castle Green, stands a well-known statue of Robin Hood, sculpted by James Woodford in 1952.

NUN BETTER In John Owen Smith's pantomine *Robin Hood* (1990), this character is described as the "genetic sister" of Friar Tuck.

NYMPHALINE A nymph who guarded the outlaw race in the early Robin Hood pantomime *Robin Hood and Richard Coeur de Lion* (?1846).

NYNEVE This is the character found in Arthurian romance, more commonly in the forms Nimue or Vivien. She imprisoned Merlin in a rock. In Yershon's *Robin Hood* (1966), she had imprisoned Merlin in an oak tree, from which he was at length released. In this play she was also the mother of the witch Maudlin who appeared in Ben Jonson's *The Sad Shepherd*.

O

ODIN Chief god of the Norse. Because he was sometimes known as *Grimnir*, the hooded one, it has been suggested he may lie behind at least part of the picture of Robin Hood. Certainly, there was much Norse settlement in the Yorkshire area in the Viking era, which could have contributed to the Robin Hood tradition.

OLIVIA A married woman, formerly affianced to Robin but since having married Nicholas, in NARH. Nicholas was captured by Prince John's underlings, but Robin rescued him. Later, after Nicholas' death, she led a rebellion, but was almost hoodwinked by the two-faced Major Tumble.

OLWYN A wizard in NARH. He told Robin he was the chosen one and filled a role not unlike that of Herne in ROS. He had been trained by Merlin (?6th Century), so he was somewhat long in the tooth by the time of Richard I. He had an assistant named Rowena, who seemed somewhat scatty for a sorceress. On one occasion Olwyn had to join forces with Prince John's witch Mortiana to defeat the dead wizard Malenoch, who had acquired Merlin's sceptre and was intending to bring an army of the dead back to life to take over England.

OUTLAW (Latin *exlex*) The status of Robin and his followers. An outlaw was not alone hunted by law enforcers, but was denied the protection of the law. In early times this meant you could actually murder an outlaw without incurring any punishment, but so severe a view changed over the centuries. An outlaw was described as being civilly dead (*civiliter mortuus*). When a man was summoned to appear before a court and failed to do so, he was proclaimed an outlaw. In Robin Hood's case, it was sometimes said he had been summoned for non-payment of debt. There seems to have been no adequate machinery to haul an individual before the law courts. The term 'wolfshead' was applied to outlaws, for the price on an outlaw's head was the same as that on a wolf's. This system was quite inadequate and led to much disorder, which, from the time of Edward I (reigned 1272-1301) could lead to the appointment of a Commission of Trailbaston. The word *trailbaston* simply means an outlaw, literally 'cudgel carrier'.

OWEN OF CLUN In ROS, an ally of Prince John, opposed to the second Robin Hood of the series. He was a great lout, a marcher lord on the Welsh border, descended from Normans settled there to keep the Welsh at bay. He wished to wed Marian and had persuaded his wizard

Gulnar to enchant her so she would acquiesce, but Robin rescued her and Owen was killed when his portcullis fell on him.

P

PANTOMIME A presentation on the British stage at the Christmas season. The pantomime originally grew out of the Harlequinade, which was formerly presented at this season. The Harlequinade in days gone by was followed by an acted fairy tale. In due course the Harlequinade disappeared and the fairy tale became the main part of the performance. While not invariably the case, the pantomime would contain a Dame (a woman of a certain age played by a man) and a principal boy played by a young woman. This was probably because in many of the original plays the character was actually a boy and had to be performed by a person with voice unbroken.

Robin Hood has been the subject of many pantomimes and instances from a few of these have been included in the text. In addition, Robin has often featured in pantomime versions of *Babes in the Wood*, in which he rescues the unfortunate children.

PAPPLEWICK A village in Sherwood Forest. It was in the church here that Alan-a-Dale's marriage was said to have occurred. In the church today there are gravestones with carvings of bows and arrows.

PEDLAR Character in the ballad *The Bold Pedlar and Robin Hood.* He is identical with Gambol Green; for information *see* **Gambol Green**. This ballad should not be confused with *Robin Hood and the Pedlars* for which *see* **Pedlars.**

PEDLARS In the ballad *Robin Hood and the Pedlars*, Robin Hood, Will Scarlet and Little John stopped some pedlars, one of whom was called Kit o' Thirsk. They had a quarterstaff fight with them until Kit knocked Robin out. Little John and Will thought Robin dead, but Kit said he would cure him by giving him a balsam, which he put in his mouth. When the pedlars had departed, Robin came to and vomited the balsam over his companions, so they

"Had their faces besmeared, both eyes and beard
Therewith most piteously."

PEMBROKE, EARL OF The villain of *Robin Hood an Opera* (1730). He loved King Edward's sister Matilda, of whom Robin Earl of Huntingdon was enamoured. Pembroke caused Robin to become an outlaw. At the end of the opera he fell at Robin's hand.

PILLORY HOLE Skelton in his *Magnificence* (*ca.* 1500) says that certain boys would have made him preach like Friar Tuck from the pillory hole. This would indicate that there was some lost tradition that the goodly friar was placed in the pillory, but that this did not quench his homiletic ability and he was able to mouth a sermon in that uncomfortable situation.

PIRATES Robin Hood had two notable encounters with pirates. In the ballad NN, Robin once went to Scarborough and, using the name Simon-over-the-Lee, enlisted on a fishing vessel with a view to earning money. Perhaps things were slow in the robbery business. He proved absolutely hopeless at fishing, much to the mirth of the fishermen. Then French pirates came into sight. Robin had himself bound to the mast and, with his bow, he picked off the pirates one by one. The fishermen seized their gold and gave it to Robin, who used it to make an habitation for the oppressed.

Another tale relates how Robin and his men defeated Danish pirates at Whitby. The Danes sought to climb the cliffs, but Robin and his men rolled boulders down upon them and, after the boulders, rained arrows, completely defeating them. Although nine outlaws perished, seventy pirates bit the dust.

PLUCK BUFFET A medieval game. One shot at a target and, if one missed, one received a blow. In the *Gest*, when King Edward visited Robin they played this game. Robin and the King played it as they made their way to Nottingham afterwards.

PLUMPTON PARK Here King Edward in the *Gest* found Robin had killed his deer. R. Holt thinks Plumpton Park is identical with Plumton Wood in the Fylde (Lancashire), rather than the park of the same name in Cumbria. Another possibility was a Plumpton Park in Yorkshire near Knaresborough.

PONTEFRACT A Yorkshire town. Here, according to legend, Robin was proclaimed an outlaw.

POPE DE LOCKSLEY, JOHN A luminary of the London Robin Hood Society, he claims to be a modern descendant of Robin Hood.

POTTER Protagonist of the ballad RHP. A play called *Robin Hood and the Potter* (16th Century) also appeared.

The Potter, on his way through the forest, was asked by Robin to pay for his passage through the woodland, but declined. In the play he was accompanied by a boy named Jack. Robin and he began to fight, Robin armed with a sword and he with a staff. The Potter proved the victor, striking Robin on the neck. After this violent confrontation, outlaw and Potter seem to have got along quite well. Robin borrowed the Potter's clothes, took his pots and went into Nottingham. There he sold the pots far too cheaply and gave those unsold to the Sheriff's wife. She invited him to dine with herself and her husband. (The Sheriff actually lived in a house in Nottingham, not in the castle itself). Afterwards Robin distinguished himself in an archery contest with the Sheriff's men and told the Sheriff he had often competed with Robin Hood. This excited the Sheriff wondrously and Robin told him he would bring him to meet Robin Hood on the morrow. He took the Sheriff to the forest and winded his horn, whereupon Little John appeared. The Sheriff was now a prisoner, but Robin let him go, sending with him a palfrey for his wife. When the Sheriff revealed to his wife what had happened, she "took up a loud laughing," and who can blame her?

Robin gave the Potter ten pounds for his wares and they parted on good terms.

PRINCESS An anonymous English Princess in PA, whose hand was sought by the Prince of Aragon; *see* **Aragon, Prince of.**

PROVERBS A number of proverbs are sayings about Robin Hood. A selection is given below:

(1) *Robin Hood robbed the rich and gave to the poor.* This is perhaps the best-known
    one, but traditionally it was never uttered in so many words. Stowe said, "Poor
    men's goods he spared, abundantly relieving them with that which by theft he got
    from abbeys and the houses of rich carls." "These took from the rich to give the

poor," writes William Warner in *Albion's England* (1589). John Taylor the Water
Poet had much the same to say:

> "And Robin Hood with Little John agreed
> To rob the rich men and the poor to feed".
> *-An Arrant Thief*

(1623).

(2) Many speak of Robin Hood that never bent his bow, i.e., many talk of things of
which they have no experience. There are a number of verbal variants of this
proverb.

(3) Robin Hood could bear any wind but a thaw wind.

(4) Robin Hood's mile, i.e., a mile far longer than a normal mile.

(5) Robin Hood's pennyworths i.e. goods sold cheaply; *see* articles **Butcher, Potter.**

(6) To go round Robin Hood's barn, i.e., to take the long way to anywhere.

(7) To overshoot Robin Hood, i.e., to make a claim far greater than warranted.

PUCK *see* **Robin Goodfellow.**

PUCK-HAIRY The spirit who aided the witch Maudlin in *The Sad Shepherd.* One wonders if he is supposed to be identical with the Puck of Shakepeare's *Midsummer Night's Dream.* While Puck may originally have been a generic name for a type of fairy, Shakespeare makes him an individual being, identical with Robin Goodfellow. However, Jonson's Puck-hairy may be connected with Pickelharing, who appears in a number of German dramas.

Q

QUEEN, SIR ROBERT A secret son of Robin Hood according to the *Green Arrow* comic series.

QUICKFOOT A name given by the British press to a yeti-like figure reported in Britain from time to time. The name is given by analogy with the American bigfoot. Sightings have been reported in South-West England and Scotland. Recently there have also been sightings in Sherwood Forest and it has been argued that a population of such creatures dwelling there in times gone by may have fed or been the origin of the Robin Hood legend. It seems unlikely a large anthropoid or humanoid could have survived undetected all these years in a country the size of Britain. A forthcoming book on the subject by Jonathan Downes may shed more light on the matter.

R

RABBIE HOODS According to a theory advanced by S. Knight, this character, a Scotsman, was the original Robin Hood.

RAGGED ROBIN A plant known as Robin Hood in the dialects of Devon and Dorset.

RALPH DE MONTFAUCUN Sheriff of Nottingham in Peacock's *Maid Marian* (1822).

RANDOLF, EARL OF CHESTER An historical personage who held this title from 1181-1232. He is mentioned in *Piers Plowman* together with Robin Hood, as one of the characters says he can repeat rhymes of both. *Piers Plowman* dates from about 1380. It has been suggested that, as Randolf was historical, so must Robin have been, but the inference is not justified, nor does their being mentioned together necessarily mean they were contemporaries. H. Bett notes an interesting tradition that a mob of minstrels once rescued Randolf from prison. For his connection with Fulk Fitzwarin, a possible prototype of Robin Hood, *see* **Fulk Fitzwarin.**

RANGER An anonymous forester who fought with Robin and then joined his band in the ballad *Robin Hood and the Ranger.*

RANULF A representative of Prince John in the film *Robin and Marian* (1976). Also the name of William I's chancellor and Robin's inveterate foe in Park Godwin's *Robin and the King* (1973).

RED FRIAR In LS, a worthy opponent of Little John who claimed to have power from the Pope to put the outlaws down.

RED ROGER *see* **Roger of Doncaster.**

RED TOM In Emery's *Tales of Robin Hood* (1988), a member of Robin's band who was also a carpenter. His wife, not caring to live among outlaws, had deserted him. His daughter, Polly, remained with him.

REYNOLD GREENLEAF The alias under which Little John took service with the Sheriff. Although this is related in the *Gest*, elsewhere is the same poem *Reynold* is mentioned, apparently as a separate character. In RHLJ, Reynold Greenleaf is a member of the band distinct from Little John.

RICHARD I, called "the Lionheart" King of England 1189-1199. Before his coronation, he twice rebelled against his father, Henry II. In the entirety of his reign, he spent only six months in England. He departed on the Third Crusade in 1190 and conquered Cyprus from its emperor, Isaac Comnenus (who had declared independence from the Byzantine Empire), on the way. In Cyprus, he married Berengaria, daughter of Sancho VI of Navarre. Richard was rumoured to be homosexual and was even said to have married Berengaria because she resembled her brother, but the first statement is unproven, the second downright unlikely. His efforts on Crusade were not entirely successful, for, while he captured Acre, he failed to do likewise with Jerusalem. He returned incognito, but was captured by Duke Leopold of Austria on the way and then handed over to the Holy Roman Emperor (i.e., the ruler of Germany), who demanded a ransom for his release. He returned to England in 1194. His brother John had taken over a number of castles, but all capitulated at once save Nottingham, which he had to capture. He tried John in the Great Hall there and banished him, but this sentence was revoked..

The first writer to place Robin Hood in the reign of Richard I was the Scottish chronicler John Major in his *Historia Majoris Britanniae* (1521). In Scott's *Ivanhoe* (1818), he is the returning king, who will set all things right. In later retellings and films, Robin and his men are depicted, not so much as bandits, but as partisans, resistance fighters upholding Richard's cause against the pretensions of the wily Prince John. However, it must not be forgotten that Robin was not always seen in this light. Although ROS places Robin's early career in the reign of

Richard, it is careful to show him not as one who seeks to maintain Richard's power and Richard himself is portrayed as treacherous and underhand.

The meeting between Richard and Robin in the forest is treated somewhat differently in the ballad KD, where there is no reference to Richard's having been on Crusade or in captivity. He was, according to this account, a normal ruler and Robin a normal lawbreaker. It says that Richard and his retinue went into the forest disguised as monks. They were stopped by Robin and his band, but Richard claimed to be the King's messenger, for Robin invited him to dinner. The King was impressed by the demeanour of Robin's men, feeling they could teach those at court a thing or two. When at last he revealed his identity, Richard gave Robin and the outlaws a pardon and the whole band advanced on Nottingham.

As this crowd were seen approaching by the good burghers of Nottingham, they feared the King had been slain and that Robin and his company were come to take over the city. They rushed to see what would happen next. The ballad states:

> "The ploughman left his plough in the fields,
> The smith ran from his shop.
> Old folks also that scarce could go
> Over their sticks did hop."

The Sheriff then had to entertain Robin and Richard to dinner and then all departed for London.

In GA also Richard is shown, not as an absent king, but as one who is quite determined that this outlaw Robin Hood in the north country will be brought to book .

The image of Richard now, however, particularly after a spate of films, is that of one only too glad that Robin had been thwarting Prince John, the Sheriff and anyone else who needed a bit of a thwart in his absence and this is the notion that remains in the popular consciousness.

RICHARD, EARL Robin's grandfather in the ballad BRH.

RICHARD-ATTE-LEE We first encounter this character in the *Gest* as he made his way through the forest and he was in a state that makes *woebegone* an inadequate word. We are told that

> "All dreary was his semblance
> And little was his pride.
> His one foot in the stirrup stood,
> The other waved beside.
>
> His hood hanged in his eyen two
> He rode in simple array,
> A sorrier man than he was one
> Rode never in summer day."

Even the most unobservant could tell this individual was unlikely to prove the life and soul of the party, even supposing he were invited to one. He came of an old respected family, who had been knights for a hundred years, but his son had killed a knight and squire in a joust. To obtain the son's pardon he had had to borrow £400 from the Abbot of St Mary's, his lands being held as security. This was the very day the repayment was due and he didn't have the money. He was lucky to run into Robin Hood and his merry company, who lent him the money, not to mention a horse and a palfrey. Little John was to accompany him as his squire. It would be unworthy to suspect that Little John was sent with him to ascertain that his tale was true and that he wasn't going to head for the nearest tavern and whoop it up with the £400.

The story, of course, was all too true. The Abbot wanted those lands and was sure Sir Richard would not have the wherewithal. The Prior, who seems to have been a true Christian, was not happy about all this at all, but the Abbot, having seniority, quashed his objections. At first Sir Richard pretended he didn't have the money and asked for an extension of the loan. The Abbot wasn't having any of this. Then Richard produced the money to the Abbot's chagrin and returned home with his wife to Verysdale.

On the day he was to repay Robin, he turned up a little late and apologised. Robin said not to worry. He had asked the loan in the name of the Virgin Mary, for whom Robin had a special reverence and, as it happened, the High Cellar of St Mary's Abbey had been relieved of £800 by Robin earlier that day, so St Mary had repaid the loan and added a good deal more.

When Robin and his band were ambushed at the archery contest given by the Sheriff, Sir Richard gave them refuge. Sir Richard was captured subsequently by the Sheriff's men, but rescued by Robin and brought to the greenwood.

This knight as 'Sir Richard Lea' is Marian's father in Tennyson's *The Foresters*; as 'Richard Leaford' he is Marian's father in ROS.

As to whether there is an historical personage behind Sir Richard, P.V. Harris traces a Richard of the Lea who was involved in a legal wrangle in 1317, while J. Bellamy mentions a Richard de la Lee, a priest, as a candidate. Another possibility is a Sir Richard de Thornhill who was in trouble in 1274 for breaking hunting laws. This knight lived at Thornhill Lees near Huddersfield. For the interesting theories of T. Molyneaux-Smith, *see* **Wellow.**

RICHMOND PARK A park in Surrey, which has both a Robin Hood Gate leading into it and a Robin Hood Walk inside it. This is perhaps as a result of Robin Hood May Games held there.

RITSON, ROLAND A thoroughgoing scoundrel in RHLJ. According to this, his brother-in-law was Gilbert Hood, Robin's adoptive father. He had undertaken a false marriage with Gilbert's sister (the "officiating cleric" was not what he seemed to be) and subsequently murdered her. As the servant of Philip Fitzooth, he had hidden the true Earl of Huntingdon, a baby, by prevailing on Gilbert, who was married to his sister Margaret, to raise the boy, so that the said Philip Fitzooth, the boy's great-uncle, could inherit the title. He confessed all this to Gilbert, as he felt death approaching and suspected he would soon be moving on to warmer climes.

The use of the name *Ritson* is probably an in-joke, as Ritson was the name of a collector of Robin Hood ballads and author of a life of the outlaw..

ROBERDSMEN A general term once used for outlaws which Sir Edward Cook derives from Robin Hood. It is found as early as the time of Edward I (reigned 1272-1307) in whose thirteenth statute it is mentioned.

ROBERT DE RAINAULT The Sheriff of Nottingham in ROS. He killed Robin's father to obtain the Silver Arrow.

ROBERT HOOD The name of a servant of the Abbot of Cirencester who killed someone in the Abbot's garden between 1213 and 1216. He is a possible but unlikely candidate for the real Robin Hood.

ROBERT OF HUNTINGDON The son of Robin Hood in the film *Bandit of Sherwood Forest* (1946).

ROBERT OF HUNTINGTON born ?1180. The son of David Earl Lennox, second Earl of Huntington by his wife,

Matilda of Chester. The Huntington here is likely to be the place so called in Yorkshire.

David was succeeded by Robert's younger brother John the Scot. Fordun claimed Robert had died in infancy. However, the question has been posed as to whether he really did or went on to become Robin Hood, true Earl, not of Huntingdon, but of Huntington.

ROBIN 1 The name of the son of Robin Hood in the film *Rogues of Sherwood Forest* (1950). Prince John had, by this time, ascended the throne and young Robin was one of those who prevailed on him to sign Magna Carta.
2 The name of Robin and Marian's son in Barbara Green's story *Marion's Christmas Rose* (1984).

ROBIN AND GANDELYN Heroes of a ballad of the same name. Both were poachers. Robin was shot dead by the forester Wrennock, who was then shot by Gandelyn. It has been suggested that Robin was one of the prototypes out of which the character of Robin Hood grew.

ROBIN DES BOIS The French form of Robin Hood, meaning 'Robin of the Woods'. It has been suggested that this character was the true origin of Robin Hood, introduced into England with the French *pastourelles.* At any rate, he became definitely identified with Robin after the two adaptations into French of RHLJ, attributed to the elder Dumas, in the 19th Century. E. Cobham Brewer avers this personage is known in German lore and, if so, he may be connected with Knecht Ruprecht, details of whom are to be found in the present writer's *Handbook of Fairies* (1998).

ROBIN GOODFELLOW A tricksome sprite in English folklore who, feels J. Grimm, has somehow become mixed up with Robin Hood, though Grimm adduces scant material in favour of this.. He obviously thought Robin Hood some kind of woodsprite. Certainly the name Robin was applied, not alone to Robin Goodfellow, but also to the similar Robin Roundcap, found in the vicinity of Haliwell. Grimm also feels there may be a connection with a German sprite named Hodekin, who was to be found near Hildesheim. However, in the original sources, no magical or spritish powers are ascribed to Robin, which argues against his being the same character. In Shakespeare's *Midsummer Night's Dream*, Robin Goodfellow is identified with Puck, but Puck may have been a species name rather than that of an individual. Under the name of Puck he appears in Emery's *Tales of Robin Hood* (1988), where he helps Robin.

ROBIN HOOD When we come to consider the personage who is the focus of this work, it is hard to produce a cohesive biography. Our major sources of information about him lie in ballads. These ballads doubtless contain stories gleaned from earlier ballads, now lost, and traditions. Whether these ballads and traditions were inspired by an historical person, a literary invention or a mythological being is still open to question.

The longest ballad featuring our hero is *A Little Gest of Robin Hood* (late 15th Century). This tells how Robin succoured the unfortunate knight, Sir Richard-atte-Lee; how Little John became the Sheriff's servant and enabled Robin to capture him; how Robin and his men entered the Sheriff's archery contest and thereafter had to flee to Sir Richard's castle; how King Edward came to Sherwood and pardoned Robin; how Robin returned to the greenwood and was eventually killed by the Prioress of Kirklees. It has been suggested that the composer of this work simply strung a number of discrete ballads together, but modern criticism inclines to the belief that its anonymous author was familiar with the contents of earlier ballads and used them, but that the versification was his own.

Other ballads yield further information about Robin. They tell how he met with Little John and Friar Tuck, fought Guy of Gisborne, encountered pirates, etc. They are generally vague about the reason for his outlawry – there is a suggestion that it was because of debt, a not infrequent reason for outlawry in those days. In *Robin Hood's Progress to Nottingham*, however, we are told that, at the age of fifteen, he bet certain foresters he could slay a deer. He won the bet, but they failed to pay up, so he murdered them, thus becoming a wanted man. When the characters of Robin and Marion apperared in the French pastourelles, Robin was possibly identified with Robin Hood and Marion became the Maid Marian of the Robin Hood legend.

Whether he resided mainly in Barnsdale or Sherwood is a matter of controversy addressed in the articles on those forests. The question of his historicity has exercised many a wit and records have been scoured to find possible references to him. F.G. Child was adamant that he was a balladeers' figment. Lord Raglan was sure he originated in the May Games and that the tales of his adventures arose subsequently. The first time we find an actual mention of him is in *Piers Plowman* (14th Century) and it has been maintained he could have lived only a couple of generations previously to have survived in oral tradition. This perhaps underestimates the strength of folk memory in non-literate communities. It is true, however, that he is often mentioned after 1377, though not before. Nevertheless, there are clues that he was known earlier: in 1262 the name 'Robehod' was applied to William le Fevre in Berkshire, as though this were some generic term for an outlaw, borrowed from some earlier prototype.

Historians have sought to link Robin with Edward II, who is a likely candidate for the King Edward of the *Gest*, especially as he is known to have made a progress to the north. After this progress, a Robin Hood was found in his service. An objection is that this name also occurs in the records of Edward's household before the progress was made. This can be overridden by pointing out that Edward made an earlier visit to the north in February/March 1323 and he could then have enlisted this Robin in his service. Unfortunately, this Robin seems somewhat feeble for the outlaw. He left Edward's service in 1324 because he could no longer work, presumably because of ill health or decrepitude.

Another candidate put forward for Robin is a Robert Hood, who is mentioned with his wife Matilda, in the Wakefield Court Rolls of 1316 and 1317. There is no evidence, however, that this individual ever became an outlaw. The notion that Matilda was the "real" name of Marian is a late intrusion into the legend, perhaps no older than the 16th Century.

In fact, the use of *Robehod* for William le Fevre implies an earlier Robin Hood and such a notion is further buttressed by the appearance of a surname "Robynhood" as though given in reverence to such an outlaw. This surname is recorded in Sussex in 1269, which would suggest that the figure of the outlaw had by then grown in popular imagination. An outlaw who could have inspired such popularity is one Robert Hood or Hobbehod, who is mentioned in 1228, 1230 and 1231. Phillips and Keatman have argued that the career of Fulk Fitzwarin (q.v.) contributed much to the legend, but that the original Robin Hood was Robert FitzOdo of Loxley in Warwickshire; *see* **Locksley**.

As to the dates which early historians assign Robin, the Scotsman John Major (died 1550) places him firmly in the reign of Richard I (1189-99), while Andrew of Wyntoun (*ca.* 1350-*ca.* 1435) says Robin and Little John were outlaws in 1283-5, when Edward I was on the throne. Walter Bower's continuation of John of Fordun's

Scotichronicon (*ca.* 1440) claims that Robin was a famous outlaw in 1366, when Henry III was king. The Sloan MS places his birth in 1160, while Throsby in *Ducatus Leodensis* asserts he died in 1247. All this merely highlights the confusion about when, if ever, he flourished.

Another question is whether he was first conceived as a yeoman or an outlawed nobleman. The idea that he was a nobleman may not antedate *DownfallREH*, though Grafton, in his *Chronicle*, notes a curious tradition that he was born into the lower classes, ennobled and subsequently lost his title.

Regarding Robin's birth, BBVM avers his father was a forester who had outshot the famous outlaws Adam Bell, Clym of the Clough and William of Cloudesley. In A. Smith's *History of Highwaymen* (1714), we are assured that his family were shepherds and he started life as a butcher. A detailed account comes from the Scottish ballad BRH. Here we learn his mother was Earl Richard's daughter, his father was called Willie and Robin was conceived out of wedlock. His unfortunate mother fled to the forest, where she gave birth. Her father's men found her there. Her father accepted the child, saying:

"And Robin Hood in the good greenwood
And that shall be his name."

In Parker we are told that Robin was the Earl of Huntingdon, driven into outlawry because of money owed to the Abbot of St Mary's. Parker also asserts that it was a friar, rather than the Prioress of Kirklees, who bled Robin to death.

Robin is generally depicted as courteous, though this could indicate either yeomanly or gentle birth. It has been claimed that the idea of his robbing the rich to give to the poor is late, but his instructions to his followers in the *Gest* indicate a generally benevolent attitude. Camden describes him as the 'gentlest of thieves' and Major says he was 'humane'. This is echoed in such quotations as:

> "These took from the rich to give to the poor"
> -----William Warner, *Albion's England* (1589).

> "And Robin Hood and Little John agreed
> To rob the rich men and the poor to feed".
> -----John Taylor The water Poet, *An Arrant Thief* (1622).

> "He was a merry rather than a mischievous thief"
> -----Thomas Fuller, *Worthies of England* (1662).

All this, of course, does not mean that, if there was an historical Robin Hood, he was the benevolent personage later literature was to make him. The picture of his being a sort of partisan of the absent King Richard is, in particular, doubtful; but it is surely the Robin Hood of legend and literature that has exercised such appeal to the public down through the centuries.

ROBIN HOOD A famous song which was the theme of the Sapphire Films television series *Robin Hood,* telling of our hero's riding through the glen with his band of followers. It was written by Carl Sigman (1909-2000).

ROBIN HOOD The name of three villages in England – one near Chesterfield, one near Wigan and one near Leeds. A hill on the Shap Fells in Cumbria also bears the hero's name. It has also been given to overseas towns, one in the United States and one in Australia.. There was formerly a place so called in Newfoundland, but it changed its name to Port Rexton. Although Ireland has no association with Robin, there is a Robin Hood Estate in the environs of Dublin.

ROBIN HOOD The name of a hat, called after the outlaw, but worn by females. Its name may be due to the fact that one of its essential components is a feather.

ROBIN HOOD A remote ostlery at Stannington in the Peak District. It is noted for its Hallowe'en celebrations.

ROBIN HOOD DAY May 6th is to be declared Robin Hood Day in Waynesville, North Carolina, and there will be an associated festival.

ROBIN HOOD FAIRE An annual event which takes place at Robin Hood Castle in Gloucester, Massachussetts.

ROBIN HOOD FESTIVAL An event held annually in Sherwood Forest. There have been eighteen of them to date.

ROBIN HOOD HILLS These are situated near Annesley (Nottinghamshire). and contain a large rock known as Robin Hood's Seat.

ROBIN HOOD LAND A festival in Austria based on the Robin Hood legend. It will be centred on the village of Donnerswachbald.

ROBIN HOOD PAGEANT This is an annual medieval pageant held in Nottingham.

ROBIN HOOD WOOD A wood in Kent which bears the name of the outlaw. In recent times there has been a report of a peculiar creature dwelling there – a gigantic white rabbit. This, presumably, has no connection with our hero.

ROBIN HOODER In the Spen Valley, a name for the south-east wind.

ROBIN HOODNIK The hero of the cartoon film of the same name produced by Hanna-Barbera in 1972. Here the characters of the legend are depicted as animals, Robin Hoodnik himself being a dog.

ROBIN HOOD'S ARBOUR An earthwork in Berkshire, formerly known as Robin
Hood's Bower.

ROBIN HOOD'S BARN A term once used to mean a far-flung place. The saying *To go by Robin Hood's Barn* meant to take the long way in making a journey.

ROBIN HOOD'S BAY A place in Yorkshire, perhaps the area from where Robin was supposed to have set sail when he fought the French pirates. It received its present name in the 16th Century. Before this it was known as Fylingthorpe.

ROBIN HOOD'S BED Part of Blackstone Edge in the Pennines, near Rochdale.

ROBIN HOOD'S BOG A marshy area in Chillingham Park, Northumberland. No one seems to know how it came to be connected with the outlaw.

ROBIN HOOD'S BUTT **1** In Shropshire, one of a number of Bronze Age burial mounds is so called. Robin is supposed to have climbed up a tree in it to shoot his arrow at Ludlow Church.

2 On the Portway, an ancient track on the Long Mynd in Shropshire, stand two mounds, each called Robin Hood's Butt.
3 In Cumbria there is a Robin Hood's Butte.

ROBIN HOOD'S BUTTS A pair of hills in Herefordshire. According to one legend about them, Robin and Little John, being of an anticlerical bent, were each carrying a spadeful of mould to destroy the monks at Wormsley. A cobbler spied them on their way. They asked him how far it was to their destination and the cobbler replied that, if he gave them all the shoes he had and more besides, they would wear them out before reaching the place. Grumpily, Little John and Robin dumped the two lumps of mould there and they became the hills. An alternative version states the hills were the work of the Devil and were called after the famous outlaw because, when he stood on one of them, he could strike a tree with an arrow on the other.

Other places have also borne this name – in Dorset, Cheshire, Shropshire, Somerset and Yorkshire (which has three of them). Butts were elevations behind targets which prevented arrows from going astray.

ROBIN HOOD'S CAVE 1 A cave amongst Cresswell Crags, Nottinghamshire, which, presumably, the outlaw was thought to have frequented. The cave has been in use since prehistoric times: remains of Neanderthal man dated to 60,000 years ago have been found there.
2 A little cave near the River Maun. In days gone by it may have been of greater extent, otherwise it is difficult to envisage Robin taking shelter there.

ROBIN HOOD'S CROSS 1 Mentioned as being at Pleesley (Nottinghamshire). It can no longer be identified, but in the village there remains the stump of a cross. It may have stood here.

2 This was supposed to have been on Bradwell Edge (Derbyshire). It is mentioned as *Robins Crosse* in 1319.

ROBIN HOOD'S HILL This is situated in Oxton (Nottinghamshire). It has standing on it a burial mound called Robin Hood's Pot, but this originally referred to a stone some distance westwards.

ROBIN HOOD'S LARDER A tree in Sherwood. Here Robin was supposed to have hung his venison. It was also known as the Shambles. It was blown down by severe winds in 1960.

ROBIN HOOD'S OAK This once stood on Wharncliffe Crags (Yorkshire). It is said that Robin once hid in it.

ROBIN HOOD'S PENISTONE Sleight's Pasture, a field near Halifax (Yorkshire) contains this particular monument. The story goes that Robin was on top of Sheeklesborough and, picking up the Penistone, kicked it into the distance. It split in the air, part coming down in Kelton and part in Sleight's Pasture. C. Hole adds that another rock of considerable proportions was supposed to have been tossed from his spade when he was digging on a hill.

ROBIN HOOD'S RACE A turf maze near the village of Sneinton, about four miles north-east of Nottingham. It is first mentioned in C. Deering's *History of Nottingham* (1751). It has also been referred to as St Ann's Maze and the Shepherd's Race. According to Throsby's *History of Nottinghamshire* (1797) it is said that its area was 324 square yards and its pathway 535 yards. Deering thought the maze of monkish origin, though he may have been wrong as heraldic designs called fitchees found on it are unlikely to be consistent with this. The maze was ploughed up in 1797.

ROBIN HOOD'S STABLES An artificial cave near Papplewick. Legend has it that Robin's horses, used in his robberies, were kept here.

ROBIN HOOD'S STEED According to Robert Graves, a name given to the woodlouse when it crawls out of the Yule Log.

ROBIN HOOD'S STOOP A stone pillar on Offerton Moor near Shatton, a small village. From here Robin was supposed to have shot an arrow to Hathersage Church. The distance is 1½ miles.

ROBIN HOOD'S STRIDE Two stones in Derbyshire. Here Robin stood, a foot on each, and urinated. Seven maidens who saw him turned to stone. Three of the stones remain. This is probably a story which antedates the Robin Hood tales in which Robin has taken the place of some mythological person.

ROBIN HOOD'S WELL A well, also known as St Anne's Well, it is given under its Robin Hood name (actually as *Robin Wood's Well*) in 1548, but it is probably identical with the Robynhode Well referred to in 1500. It may originally have been called the Owswell. It lies near Nottingham. In 1887 the spring was covered by a railway embankment, but it was rediscovered in 1987 by excavation. There are other wells so called: one is at Hathersage, the reputed home of Little John; one is at Fountains Abbey (Yorkshire); and one is the source of a stream south of Wensleydale.

ROBIN LONGBOW The original name of Robin Hood in Robin McKinley's *Outlaws of Sherwood* (1988). He is depicted as a rather inept figure, not at all a good marksman, in this work.

ROBIN THE HOODED MAN The theme tune of the series ROS. It was composed by Ciaran Brennan and performed by Clannad.

ROBIN WOOD The villain in a Gloucestershire mummers' play. Whether or not he is to be identified with Robin Hood is far from certain.

ROBIN'S WOOD HILL This lies near Gloucester and has a beacon on top of it. Its earliest association with the outlaw is when it is called Robinhoodes Hill in 1624.

ROBYN HOOD 1 The heroine of the Canadian television series *Back to Sherwood Forest*. Robyn, a Canadian teenager, made the discovery that she was a descendant of Robin Hood. She also found out that, back in Merrie England, Robin and Marian were enchanted by a witch, Beren, and she had to make a number of time-travelling visits to the Middle Ages to obtain King Richard's magical gifts to free her famous ancestors. In this, she was aided by the outlaws' children – Joan Little, Alana Dale and, as a sort of token male, Phil Scarlet. Beren was in league with the Sheriff of Nottingham whose son, far from enthralled by papa's skulduggery, was happy to lend Robyn a hand.
2 The heroine of the musical *Robyn Hood: Outlaw Princess* by New Zealand composer Gary Deverne. In the story, a girl dreamt she lived out the career of Robin Hood, but as a female, not a male.

ROBYN OF SHERWOOD The daughter of Robin Hood in Paul D. Storrie's Caliber Comics series. She was a tough female warrior. King John, now enthroned, had decided that all memory of the late Robin Hood should now be obliterated. Robyn had other ideas.

ROCKET ROBIN HOOD A descendant of Robin who flourished in 3000 AD and led a band of outlaws on Sherwood Asteroid. This was all depicted on a Canadian television cartoon series produced in the 1960s.

ROCKINGHAM A royal forest where, in 1354, a man called Robin Hood was charged with trespass. Though most historians consider this personage to have lived too late to have been behind the Robin Hood story, such a position has been argued. However, it shows that by this stage such a name may have become a general appellative for lawbreakers.

ROGER GODBERD A medieval English outlaw whose exploits may have contributed somewhat to the Robin Hood legend. He operated in Sherwood Forest. When know he received a pardon in 1265, but he was an outlaw once more in 1267. There seem to have been a couple of incidents approaching battles between the Constable of Nottingham Castle and the Sherwood outlaws. Eventually Roger was captured. The last record of him is as a prisoner at Bruges.

ROGER OF DONCASTER Also referred to as *Sir Doncaster*, he was at Kirklees when Robin was killed and may have been an accomplice to the murder. In one version, under the name of Red Roger, he actually attacked the ailing Robin, but was slain by him. At least one form of the tale makes him the Prioress's lover. Various attempts have been made to identify this personage, but all are guesswork. There was a Roger de Doncaster charged with adultery in 1309; a Roger, son of William of

Doncaster, was mentioned in a court order of 1327; a Roger of Doncaster was Vicar of Ruddington in 1328; while a Roger of Donaster was imprisoned in 1333. None of these, however, is necessarily the character concerned.

ROSSEL The nickname applied to the English king William II before he became king in Park Godwin's *Robin and the King* (1973). He and Robin fell out after his coronation over the policies he then espoused, but they had been friends beforehand.

ROSSLYN CASTLE In Scotland, the seat of the Sinclairs, whose church, Rosslyn Chapel, is the focus of much attention from investigators of supposed historical mysteries. The castle boasts two towers, one called Robin Hood, the other Little John. It is probable they were given their names because of performances of Robin Hood plays nearby, perhaps given by Gypsies.

ROUND TABLE The table of King Arthur. In ROS it had survived into Robin's day. It had had a succession of guardians, each named Agravaine. The present Agravaine was dying and the voice of Arthur asked Robin to succeed him, as he had no son. Robin pointed out that Agravaine's daughter, Isadora, would do just as well and the ghostly voice of Arthur concurred.

ROWAN HOOD Daughter of Robin Hood in Nancy Springer's book of the same name (2001). Her real name was Rosemary, but, on her mother's death, she joined Robin in the forest, renaming herself. However, she did not stay with Robin but took herself off. Her companions included a seven-foot minstrel and a runaway princess. Her adventures continued in *Lionclaw* (2002).

ROWENA 1 The name of Ivanhoe's betrothed. Many readers of the book feel Ivanhoe should have married Rebecca rather than her, but such a union would not have been possible in that era. However, see **Ivanhoe** for further details.
2 A lady who, to escape an unwanted marriage, dressed as a boy to join Robin's band in Kathryn Kramer's *Lady Outlaw* (1997).
3 A benevolent and perhaps rather scatty witch in NARH.

RUBYGILL, ABBOT OF The clergyman who was to have officiated at Robin and Marian's marriage, before his outlawry, in Peacock's *Maid Marian* (1822). When soldiers turned up and interrupted the nuptials and Robin's men fired arrows in response, the Abbot was much dismayed for, as Peacock puts it, he did not want to change from a ghostly friar into a friarly ghost.

S

SABINA A companion of Marian in Scott Lynch-Giddings' *A Fancyfull Historie of Robin Hood* . This play, though modern, is written in Shakespearean style and fashion.

ST EDMUND'S BALK A ridge in Huntingdon. Two standing stones grace it, with nicks at the top, as though they had been grazed by arrows. These stones are called Robin Hood and Little John. These two worthies are said to have shot arrows here from Alwalton Churchyard.

ST MARY'S ABBEY Situated in York, it was to the abbot of this establishment that the morose Sir Richard-atte-Lee owed money. According to Parker, the abbot (perhaps a predecessor) seized Robin's lands in payment for debt, thus forcing him into outlawry. He later captured the abbot, forced him to say Mass for the outlaws, then placed him backwards on a horse and sent him away. On another occasion, Robin defeated a force of 500 men sent against him by the abbot. The prototype of this abbot could have been Thomas de Multon, in office 1328-1359, well-known as a moneylender. In ROS the abbot was Hugo, the Sheriff of Nottingham's brother.

ST MARY'S CHURCH The church in Nottingham where Robin went to pray and was observed by the monk who betrayed him. The present church dates only from 1474, but may have been built on the site of an older structure. There was certainly a church in this location at the time of Domesday Book (1086), but that was destroyed in the 12th Century. The recent discovery of a secret passage from the church seems unrelated to any known Robin Hood legend.

ST MICHAEL'S CHURCHYARD There was a tradition that Robin and his followers killed thirteen people and buried them here. Around the year 1832 an excavation revealed a number of skeletons which were held to confirm the legend.

SAXONS Robin's band is oftentimes represented as a group of Saxons reacting to or resisting Norman oppression. The term *Saxon* was used generally to designate those groups of various Germanic origins who had settled in Britain in the 5th Century, displacing or subsuming the ancient Britons, who continued to exist in the west, becoming the ancestors of the Welsh and Cornish. They ruled the country until the last Saxon king, Harold II, was killed at the Battle of Hastings (1066). The Norman duke, William II, now became King William I of England. Hence there was some enmity between Saxon native and Norman conqueror, but how long this lasted is a matter of some disagreement and whether it persisted into the various times in which Robin Hood has been placed is doubtful.

SAYLIS A placename mentioned in the *Gest*. It has been identified with Sales, a medieval plantation mentioned elsewhere. This is generally held to be identical with the modern Sayle's Plantation, on the northern border of Barnsdale, just east of Wentbridge. Its existence goes some way to establishing the wood known as Barnsdale with the original Barnsdale of the Robin Hood tradition.

SCARLET, WILL One of the most well-known members of Robin's band, his name appears in a variety of forms, such as Scathlock, Scadlock and Scarlock. He is represented sometimes as Robin's nephew and is identical with the character of Gambol Green.

Will's surname was Gamwell. In the ballad RHS, Robin chanced upon him in the forest. However, when he identified himself and it transpired that he had had to flee to the forest for killing his father's steward, Robin invited him to join the band. In PA he married a daughter of the King of England, but the opera *Robin Hood* (1782) he had a likelier lover named Stella. He is supposed to be buried at Blidworth.

As to the origin of his outlaw name, it says in the ballad *Robin Hood Newly Revived* that his "stockings like scarlet shone" and this supplied his name. In RHLJ, he earned his name from his ruddy complexion. In the film *Robin Hood Prince of Thieves*, he turned out to be Robin's half-brother. In Parke Godwin's *Sherwood* (1991), he was Welsh and originally a slave. In RHLJ he is given a great many brothers and two sisters. In Clayton Emery's *Tales of Robin Hood* (1988) we are introduced to his mother, Old Bess, his son, Tam, and his daughter, Katie. In that volume, though apparently dying of gangrene, he was magically restored.

Though there is little if any doubt that Will Scarlet and Will Scathelock are the same person, the fact that the names "Scarlock" and "Scathlock" both exist in the *Gest* may indicate they started bifurcating by 1500 and in *DownfallREH* they are definitely two separate characters, brothers, sons of the Widow Scarlet. In the Sapphire Films *Robin Hood* television series, they are completely distinct. Scathelock was head of the outlaw band when Robin joined it and, mortally wounded, named Robin as his successor, while Will Scarlet joined the band later.

S.O. Addy suggested Scathelock had a mythological origin, connecting him with Loki, the trickster god of the Norse, but the present writer views this as very unlikely.

SCATHELOCK, WILL *see* **Scarlet, Will.**

SCOTCHMAN The term *Scotchman* is not really acceptable English and Scots find it distasteful (it should really be *Scotsman*), but the character so-called appears in two variant forms of a ballad, RHSc. In one ballad Robin led his band north when he went "to fight and recover his right", whatever that may have been. The Scotchman led his men against Robin, but the fighting was so ferocious that he wished he were at home with his wife. The outcome of the battle was vague. In another version, Robin met the Scotchman who wanted to join his band. Robin said he would have to test his fighting skills. They had a single combat lasting over two hours, after which the Caledonian was admitted to Robin's company.

SCOTLAND Although Scotland is rarely mentioned in Robin Hood lore, the legend seems to have been very popular there, at least from the late 1400s. In 1555 the Scottish Parliament passed an act forbidding Robin Hood plays. S. Knight has argued in favour of Robin's original being a Scotsman named Rabbie Hoods and there has been an attempt to identify Robin with the celebrated Scottish leader, Sir William Wallace.

SHADOW-OF-A-LEAF A fool in Noyes' *Robin Hood* (1926). He had his wits taken from him by Bramble, a sprite, so that he might have access to the faerie world and communicate with its inhabitants and he found this much more palatable than human wisdom. However, he sacrificed these attributes to rescue Robin when the latter was imprisoned in a dark tower. Eventually he joined Blondel in his search to find the Great King – not Richard, now dead, but Christ, who had conquered death. Shadow-of-a-Leaf is a poignant and noble character in his foolishness, which is not the folly it seems at first glance, and he rejoices that the nature of the greenwood will ultimately pull down the artificial works of man.

SHAVELDOURS With regard to Robin's being a bandit of aristocratic origin, such things were not unknown in medieval England. A friar, writing about 1317, stated that in England clergy and rustics were robbed by nobles who called themselves by the term *shaveldours*. They were also known as *ryfelours*.

SHEPHERD The protagonist of RHS, this worthy yokel was lying on the ground when Robin came by and asked him what was in his bag and bottle. The Shepherd felt this was scant concern of Robin's. The two agreed to have a fight. If the Shepherd won, he would have £20, if Robin, the bag and bottle would be his. Robin had a sword and buckler, the Shepherd but a crook, yet the latter laid into Robin so vigorously that he asked permission to blow his horn. This done, Little John appeared on the scene. He too fought the Shepherd, with no more success than Robin.

SHERIFF OF NOTTINGHAM Robin's especial foe, to whom he was constantly opposed. Because some of Robin's early adventures were set in Barnsdale, it has been suggested that he was too far away to have been involved with the Sheriff and that the Sheriff was originally the protagonist of a separate saga, independent of Robin; but, if the Yorkshire Barnsdale were indeed intended, it was sufficiently near for Robin to have been a thorn in the Sheriff's flesh without too much difficulty. Moreover, no independent ballad or tradition of the Sheriff is known.

In fact, the title 'Sheriff of Nottingham' *per se* was only created in 1449. Before that, the existing title was 'Sheriff of Nottinghamshire and Derbyshire'. As we do not know when Robin lived (if he lived at all), we cannot make more than guesses at whom the Sheriff of the ballads might be. If we opt for the time of Richard I, the sheriff in the first year of his reign was Ralph Murdoch, that in the sixth William Brewere. We do not know if there were any in between. Another possibility who has been suggested is Sir Miles de Faucunberg who was at times between 1318 and 1330 Sheriff of Nottinghamshire and Derbyshire, Sheriff of Yorkshire and Constable of Nottingham Castle. Other possibilities we might mention are Philip Mark (1209-24); Eustace of Londhan (1232-33); Sir Robert Ingran (1338-33); and John de Oxenford (*ca.* 1334-39).

Many assume the Sheriff would have lived in Nottingham Castle, but in fact he dwelt in the Red House in Angel Row.

In *DownfallREH*, the Sheriff was Warman, who had been Robin's steward before his outlawry. Robin eventually forgave him. In *Death REH* Warman refused to plot against Robin and was murdered.

As to traditional stories of the Sheriff's death, in the *Gest* he was killed by Robin when the latter was raiding Nottingham; in WTS he was hanged by Robin and his men; while in GG he was killed by a bowshot from Little John.

SHERIFF'S COOK This worthy factotum, described in the *Gest* as "a stout man and a bold", joined Robin's band. When Little John in the guise of Reynold Greenleaf had entered the Sheriff's service, he made his way to the kitchen while the Sheriff went out and helped himself to some provender. The Cook set upon him, they had a swordfight, then John invited him to join Robin's band, saying he would be paid twenty marks a year. The Cook was willing and they broke into the treasury, carrying off silver vessels and other such items.

SHERIFF'S WIFE This lady, who seems to have had a humorous turn of mind, features in P, where she laughed on hearing of the Sheriff's discomfiture. While the ballad does not give her a name, this oversight is remedied by the Dutch comic *Robin Hoed* (stories by Turk) where she was called Kunegonde. In David Stuart Ryan's *The Lost Journal of Robin Hood-Outlaw* (1989) she was called Elena and bore Robin a son.

SHERWOOD FOREST The tract of forest usually associated in the public mind with Robin. Though it is unmentioned in the *Gest,* which places him firmly in Barnsdale, the oldest reference we have associating him with a particular place is a note locating him in Sherwood. Sherwood is also his habitation in the ballad RHM, the earliest of the ballads..

In the Middle Ages Sherwood consisted of 100,000 acres. Of these 25 square miles were under tree cover, divided into coppices. It stretched from Nottingham in the south to the River Meden in the north. The River Leen formed part of its western boundary. Rivers in it included the Mann and the Rain, Day Brook and Dover Beck. The town of Mansfield lay within its limits, likewise a number of villages and two religious houses. It contained a good many areas of open ground called *dales*. It now boasts a mere 500 acres.

Game included deer and wild boar, not to mention smaller fry. Wolves would also have roved there, as several centuries were to pass before they were to be wiped out in England. Today, the forest contains over 218 species of spider and one assumes most of their ancestors were to be found there in the Middle Ages. For some time a bigfoot-like monster has been reported in the Forest. A witness claimed to have seen one cross a road about 1980, but it has featured in the news much more recently when four persons claimed to have seen a creature with glowing red eyes about eight feet from the ground. This beast is known locally as the Sherwood Forest "Thing". It has been suggested that a population of such creatures living in the forest might have helped to give rise to the Robin Hood legend.

If we have no certain evidence of Robin, we know that one outlaw at least was at large there in the 13th Century, Roger Godberd, a one time follower of Simon de Montford, who fled there after the Battle of Evesham (1265).

An early mention of Sherwood gives it the form *Scyriud* (958). After the Norman Conquest (1066), William I made it a royal forest for hunting purposes.

Sherwood Forest is now to benefit from a £5.5 million conservation scheme. It was named a national nature reserve in 2002.

SHERWOOD, CARL Inventor of a virtual reality game who brought Robin Hood characters into the real world in E. Friesner's *The Sherwood Game* (1995).

SHERWOOD FESTIVAL A Robin Hood festival held in South Africa under the aegis of the Nottingham Road Brewing Company.

SHERWOOD ROBIN HOOD FESTIVAL An annual festival held every third full week in July in Sherwood, Oregon.

SILVER ARROW A magical arrow, called Herne's arrow, in ROS. The Sheriff took it from Robin's father and later offered it as a prize in an archery contest to lure Robin out of the forest. Robin turned up disguised as an old man, Hedger of Castleton. He won the arrow, but was recognised and he and his followers had to fight their way to freedom. The story is possibly based on the ballad GA.

SILVER SWORD A mysterious person who aided Robin in Sharon Drake's *Damsel in Distress* (1992).

SIMON DE BELLEME In ROS, an evil wizard who wished to wed Marian. Later he had her kidnapped to use as bait for Robin, but Robin easily overcame him and saved Marian. de Belleme was killed by the demon whom he served.

SIMON DE VITRY In Gayle Feyrer's *Thief's Mistress* (1996), this personage was foolish enough to have Marian's mother murdered. Foolish enough, because Marian was a trained warrior and took speedy revenge.

SIMON-OVER-THE-LEE The false name used by Robin when he pretended to be a fisherman in NN.

SLIPPER, ROBIN HOOD'S W. Hutton notes in his *Journey from Birmingham to London* (1785) that he had been shown fifty years before what had been asserted to be Robin Hood's slipper at St Anne's Well near Nottingham.

STEINKOPFT, CASPER In RHLJ, one of the soldiers of the Baron of Nottingham. He had made unsavoury advances to Maude and, encountering her again, proceeded to assault her, when Robin, who had been lurking nearby, shot him through the eye, killing him.

STELLA In the opera *Robin Hood* (1782), the lover of Will Scarlet; however, because of his treacherous behaviour, he was compelled to forgo her and marry Martha.

STONE OF ROBIN HOOD The first placename on record to be called after the outlaw. Its exact location is uncertain, but it was near Barnsdale Bar in Yorkshire.

STUTELY, WILL One of Robin's band. He was once captured by the Sheriff and sentenced to the gallows. He asked the Sheriff at the time of his execution if he might be given a sword and allowed to die fighting the Sheriff's men. When this was refused, he asked if he could fight them barehanded, but the Sheriff said he must hang. This motif is found elsewhere, another instance being the Scottish song, *MacPherson's Rant.* However, Stutely was lucky, for Robin and his men staged a rescue.

In *Robin Hood an Opera* (1730), he tried to commit rape – this was not a characteristic of him in early traditions that have survived.

T

TARAGAL An evil witch in Emery's *Tales of Robin Hood* (1988). She gave Guy of Gisborne a spell to unleash an horrendous magical boar into Sherwood to destroy Robin.

THEA AELREDSON An herb woman who supported Robin in Sue Wilson's *Greenwood* (2001). The Sheriff, wounded, stumbled to her door and she healed him. This brought out a better side to the Sheriff, to whom the book is sympathetic. It also features a one-time lover of the Sheriff called Aelwynn.

THIEVES WOOD A place near Fountains Dale. It was said that certain maidens had been abducted from Mansfield, but Robin rescued them at this location.

THOMAS On the alleged gravestone of Robin Hood at Kirklees, the names of William of Goldsborough and Thomas also appeared, but whoever Thomas may have been is anybody's guess.

THORESBY HALL Situated in Sherwood, this building contains noteworthy wooden statues of Robin Hood and Little John.

THORN-WHISPER King of the Forest Sprites in Noyes' *Robin Hood* (1926).

TICKLE Marian's nurse in the Canadian pantomime *Robin Hood-a Family Musical*. This work was organised by Ross Petty and has been performed, with various changes, for at least three runs. Based on the traditional English type of pantomime, it has Nurse Tickle as its dame, i.e., a woman of a certain age played by a man.

TIME TRAVEL It is hardly surprising that Robin Hood should feature in a number of time travel science fiction stories. In the series NARH the inventor Barklay actually constructed a time machine which enabled his 20th Century descendant to visit Robin's era. There is also a type of time travel featuring Robin in the film *Time Bandits*. In the novel *The Ivanhoe Gambit* (1986) by S. Hawke, a time traveller returned to the Middle Ages to assume the persona of Richard I, intending to alter history. To prevent this, a task force was sent back into the past. They discovered an inebriate and hen-pecked Robin Hood, so one Billy Johnson replaced him and thereby the legend began. Actually, altering history by time travel would be impossible, as it would already be altered by the time the time traveller set out. Despite speculation, there is nothing to indicate that such an "altering of history" would cause a split in the historical continuum bringing two continua into being.

TINKER In the ballad T, Robin met a tinker who had a royal warrant for his arrest. Not knowing who Robin was, the Tinker decided they join forces and Robin led him into Nottinghan, where they adjourned to a tavern. Plied with drink, the Tinker fell asleep and Robin made off with the warrant and his money. On waking, the Tinker had to pay the innkeeper by handing over his working tackle. Informed by the landlord of the identity of his erstwhile companion, he set off for the greenwood, breathing fire and intent on vengeance. He encountered Robin and they had a long flight. When he was distracted, Robin sounded a mot on his horn and his followers appeared. Greatly impressed by the Tinker's prowess, Robin asked him to join his band, which he did. In RHLJ he is given a name, Gaspar-a-Tin.

TODWICK A Yorkshire village which was said to have once formed part of Sherwood Forest. An oak tree was to be found there, bearing a plaque proclaiming it to be the Trysting Tree of Robin Hood mentioned in Scott's *Ivanhoe*. It is quite possible that no one regarded it as Robin's trysting tree before the publication of Scott's novel in 1818. The oak has now been felled and replaced by bungalows for old people.

TOM FLETCHER As his name suggests, he was a maker of arrows. In ROS, he was one of the earliest members of Robin's band.

TOWZER A dog, as his name would indicate. He belonged to the Pindar of Wakefield in *Robin Hood an Opera* (1730). Little John had been improperly involved with the Pindar's wife when that worthy returned unexpectedly. John secreted himself beneath the table, pretending to be Towzer, and the deluded Pindar fed him scraps.

TRAITORS, UNLIKELY In some versions of the Robin Hood legend, unlikely personages have become traitors to Robin. One such was Will Scarlet in MacNally's *Robin Hood* (1784). Friar Tuck was working with him. The most unexpected traitor of all was Marian in Tomoyoshi Maryama's *Robin Hood* (1927).

TRAVELLER'S JOY This plant was sometimes known as Robin Hood's feather or fetter.

TRISTRAM OF GOLDSBOROUGH In the version of the story of Alan-a-Dale given in RHLJ, this was the knight crumbling with age whom Christabel, daughter of the Baron of Nottingham, was being forced to wed against her will. The Baron obtained a payment of a million marks from him in return for Christabel's hand. Naturally, Robin frustrated the whole design.

TRYSTELL TREE Allusions occur to Robin's trystell tree in the woods, obviously a meeting place. It has been suggested it was a tree which West Yorkshire County Council caused to be felled in 1961. It may also have been the Major Oak. See also **Todwick**.

V

VERYSDALE The home of Sir Richard-atte-Lee. It has been suggested it was identical with Wyresdale (Lancashire). There was a hamlet named Lee there. J. Bellamy proffers the suggestion that it was Iverishagh near Oxton, which in the 13th Century was just inside Sherwood. There is a Robin Hood Hill nearby.

W

WALLACE, WILLIAM (1272-1305) A notable Scottish patriot who not only opposed King Edward I in arms, but actually invaded England. Some have suggested that his exploits gave rise to the Robin Hood legends. It has been argued that Wallace was in love with Marion Braidfute, a knight's daughter; that his brother John equates to Little John; his monk friend John Blair to Friar Tuck; and John Balliol, the King of Scots nominated by Edward, to Prince John. Wallace is also said to have disguised himself as a potter at one time, as did Robin in P. Unfortunately, the only contemporary records of Wallace were written by the English; the Scottish records come later. It is unlikely, however, that such a one would endear himself to the English peasantry; and an English monk, contemporary with Wallace, calls him 'the Scottish Robin Hood' indicating that traditions of Robin were already known in Wallace's time.

WALTER In Tennyson's *The Foresters* (1895), the son of Sir Richard Leaford (=Sir Richard-atte-Lee) and brother of Marian. In this play, Sir Richard needed money to ransom him from the Saracens. Walter appeared at the end of the play.

WAR VETERANS It has been argued by A. Ayton that Robin and his band were military veterans. The idea stems from the fact that he came on a mention of a 'Robyn Hood' in a garrison of the Isle of Wight in 1338.

WARMAN *see* **Sheriff of Nottingham**.

WARSOP A village near Papplewick. Here it was said people never locked their doors, as Robin Hood was always welcome to drop in.

WAT O' THE WHIP In the Thriller Comics Robin Hood series and its supporting annuals, an important member of Robin's band, noted for his famous lash. His cry of *O ho ho, the whip! the whip!* doubtless appealed greatly to the juvenile audience for which these works were intended.

WATLING STREET This name was originally given to a Roman road which stretched from London to Wales. However, it was later bestowed on other roads and, when it appears in the Robin Hood ballads, this is undoubtedly the case. In 1433 the road which stretched from Ferrybridge to Worksop by way of Barnsdale was called Watling Street and this must undoubtedly be the Watling Street referred to in the *Gest*, where the outlaws encountered Sir Richard-atte-Lee.

WAYLAND A smith in Anglo-Saxon legend, perhaps originally a god. He is described as an elf, but the terms elf and god could elide into each other. He also features in continental Germanic mythology, which told how he was lamed by King Nididur and was the smith of the gods. The Saxons obviously thought he had visited England, for they called a megalithic tomb in Oxfordshire Wayland's Smithy.

In ROS, Herne gave Robin one of the seven swords forged by Wayland. A black magic group needed all seven to invoke the Devil and got hold of them, but Robin frustrated their designs.

WAYTHEMEN This is a term used of Little John and Robin Hood by Andrew of Wyntoun in his *Original Chronicle* (*ca.* 1420). It is said to mean simply men who lie in wait for potential victims, but this has been disputed.

WELLOW A village which, in the Middle Ages, lay on the north-eastern boundary of Sherwood. The lords of this area were the Foliot family. T. Molyneaux-Smith has put forward an interesting theory regarding them. He holds that they fortified the village of Wellow to protect their tenants, possibly dug escape tunnels underneath it (a dowser claimed that such tunnels exist to this day) and levied charges on those who passed through. The men of the village of Wellow were Robin Hood's "outlaws" and the head of the Foliot family was referred to as "Robin Hood". Thus the following lords of Wellow with one exception were known by this appellation:-

Robert Foliot 1110-65
Elias Foliot 1160-1220
Jordan Foliot I 1220-60
Richard Foliot I 1222-99
Jordan Foliot II 1244-99

Molyneaux-Smith further identifies Sir Richard Foliot as Sir Richard-atte-Lee and Jordan Foliot II as the Robin Hood killed by the Prioress of Kirklees.

He makes the interesting observation that the village green of Wellow was originally in the shape of an arrow pointing at Nottingham.

WERNETH LOW (Cheshire) From here Robin was supposed to have flung a rock into the River Tame. His finger marks were said to have remained on it.

WHITBY This Yorkshire town has several associations with Robin Hood. Here he is said to have defeated a contingent of Danish pirates who sought to scale the cliffs, enabling Robin and his followers to shower boulders and arrows upon them. Richard, Abbot of Whitby, was on good terms with our hero if Charlton's *History of Whitby* (1779) is to be believed. He once invited Robin and Little John to dinner. In response to his request to demonstrate their prowess with the bow, each fired an arrow from the roof of the abbey. A pillar was set up where each arrow landed. They came to earth in separate fields, which came to be known as Robin Hood's Field and Little John's Field. Each was more than a mile from the abbey.

A number of houses in the town were once known as Robin Hood's houses. In one tradition, Robin was buried at Whitby.

In Antonia Fraser's *Robin Hood* (1955), Marian's father was the Earl of Whitby.

WIDOW SCARLET In *DownfallREH*, the mother of Will Scarlet and Will Scathelock, who are treated as different characters. In Noyes' *Robin Hood* (1926), she is the mother of Will Scarlet alone. In both plays she is in sore distress over the forthcoming execution of her son(s).

WIDOW'S SONS In the ballad WTS, Robin discovered that a widow's three sons were to be hanged in Nottingham. He obtained clothes from a palmer and went into the town and offered his services to the Sheriff as a hangman. The Sheriff accepted, then Robin wound his horn and his men appeared and carried the gallows and the Sheriff into the forest, where they hanged the latter on the former. In some versions, those rescued were three squires, unconnected with any widow.

WILL O' THE GREEN An outlaw, tales of whom inspired the young Robin, in J. Walter McSpadden's *Robin Hood* (1904).

WILLIAM 1 A knight in VK. The King, tired of Robin's depredations, sent this knight with a force to capture Robin. A note was sent to our hero, demanding his surrender. He refused and a pitched battle followed, in which Sir William was slain. Neither party seems to have gained victory, but afterwards Robin, feeling ill, was bled to death by a treacherous monk.
2 Little John's brother in NARH.

WILLIAM A TRENT A soldier of the Sheriff, shot dead by Little John in GG.

WILLIAM OF CLOUDESLEY A legendary English outlaw not normally associated with Robin Hood, but with separate outlaws called Adam Bell and Clim of the Clough. However, in a poem published in 1616, William claims he shot against Robin and a number of followers in a contest. Adam Bell himself appears in a number of modern versions of the Robin Hood story.

WILLIAM OF GOLDSBOROUGH A person whose name appeared on the alleged gravestone of Robin Hood at Kirklees. Who he was is unknown, but it has been suggested that this was Will Scarlet's real name.

WILLIAM THE LION King of Scots (reigned 1165-1214). He was the Scottish king contemporary with Richard I of England and made an appearance in the

Sapphire Films television series of *Robin Hood.* Historically, his brother David was the Earl of Huntingdon.

WILLIE The father of Robin in BRH.

WILY In the play *George-a-Green* (1599), he was the pindar's servant. As George wished to wed Bettris, he had to smuggle her out of her father's home. This he did by pretending to be a woman, his face muffled because of alleged toothache. He then changed clothes with Bettris, enabling her to escape. This was before George's encounter with Robin.

WITCH OF NOTTINGHAM WELL In William Pearce's *Merry Sherwood* (1795), a benevolent sorceress who gave Robin a magic horn. She also assigned to him Harlequin as his guardian. She restored Robin to life when he had been killed.

WITCHCRAFT M.A. Murray in her books on witchcraft, argues that it was an organised pagan religion, which persisted into Christian times. Robin Hood, she maintained, was a god of the witches and his merry men were fairies, devotees of the cult rather than supernatural beings.

However, Murray's thesis is now discredited. Much of the information she adduces was extracted from supposed witches under torture and, though some referred to the Devil (whom Murray claims was really the witches' god and not the Devil of Christian belief) as Robin, the word here used may be a corruption of *rabbin*, an English word for a rabbi. The continued existence of an organised pagan cult in the Middle Ages is unsubstantiated and confessions elicited under torture must be treated, obviously, with caution. The fact that all the earliest Robin Hood sources are devoid of a supernatural element is a sure indication that he was never thought of as a divine being.

WOLF The son of Little John, rescued by Robin in the film *Robin Hood Prince of Thieves.*

WOLFSHEAD Another name for an outlaw. It came into existence because the same price was offered for an outlaw's head as was offered for a wolf's.

WOOD, CHARLIE In LS, a member of Robin's band who remained with Little John after Robin's death.

WOODWEETE An unidentified bird mentioned in GG, possibly the golden oriole (*Oriolus oriolus*).

WORMSLEY HILL A place in Herefordshire. Robin bet Little John he could jump over this hill, including its abbey. He did so, but kicked a piece out with his heel. This is now called Butt-house Knapp. Little John then leaped. He took a longer run and kicked a piece out of Canon Pyon Butt.

WORMWOOD In Gary Yershon's play *Robin Hood* (1996), Marian's aunt, who granted Marian sanctuary from Guy of Gisborne. Guy then kidnapped the unfortunate woman, but Robin and his men rescued her.

WRENTHORPE A Yorkshire village near Wakefield, which has a district that was formerly known as Robin Hood. There was a Robin Hood Farm there: the farmhouse was demolished about 1970. The Robin Hood district is referred to as Robin Hood Street Close in 1650. The village also boasted a Robin Hood Bridge and the farm had a Robin Hood Well. The hill of Potovens here was once known as Robin Hood Lane. The number of Robin Hood names in the village is puzzling and it has been suggested that here Robin had his combat with George-a-Green.

Y

YEOMAN Robin Hood is often described as a yeoman, but it is not always clear what status this title conferred. Originally it seems it signified a young man who worked in a manorial household, considered inferior to esquires, but superior to grooms; but there may be a connection with Old Friesian *gaman,* 'villager'. W.P. Ker has argued that yeomanly and knightly virtues were much the same. Certainly, this would explain the courtesy of Robin and his chivalry towards women. A yeoman at various times could mean a person in service, a journeyman, a free peasant or a small landholder.

YOUNG ROBIN HOOD A U.S. comic book hero with a secret identity. He was really a boy called Billy Lackington, who donned a Robin Hood-type costume to fight evil and was well skilled in the use of the bow. He was aided by his merry band – Freckles, Squeeky and Fatso. He first appeared in *Boy Comics* in 1942. He was sometimes teamed up with another *Boy Comics* hero, Bombshell son of War, an offspring of the god Mars.

There have been some attempts to portray Robin Hood in his youth. This includes the Young Robin Hood novels by Richard Percy and the Japanese television cartoon series *Young Robin Hood* (1990-91), called in the original Japanese *Robin Hood no Daiboka* and produced by Tatsunoko Productions. There was also *Young Robin's Hood* (2000) by Ian Whybrow and Tony Ross, which explains how Robin's band first met as children and acquired the names they were later to make famous as outlaws.

YULE LOG The log traditionally burned on the fire at Christmastide. The custom is presumably pagan in origin as Yule was the name of the midwinter feast of the Teutonic nations, its name only later being applied to Christmas.

Robert Graves maintains that the word *hood* in Robin Hood means a log and that Robin is a mythological character, originally the spirit of the Yule log. When Yule was over, he claims, Robin would shoot up the chimney and assume the form of Belin and hunt and hang Bran the wren.

This ties the story in with the custom of hunting the wren on St Stephen's Day (September 26th). This was a predominantly Celtic custom, though it seems to have been fairly well known amongst the English also. However, the names Belin and Bran seem to be taken from the Celtic gods Beli Mawr and Bran, whose name actually signified a raven, not a wren. Moreover, it is difficult to see how an Anglo-Saxon hero such as Robin could become involved with such Celtic deities.

***

A Little Gest of Robin Hood

Rendered into Modern English by Ronan Coghlan. I have not hesitated to use paraphrase and add words in the interests of rhyme and scansion, but the story remains the same. I have cheated slightly by using either 'Scathelock' or 'Scathlock' as scansion demands.

This poem is the nearest thing we have to a Robin Hood epic, including sundry adventures of the outlaw, culminating in his death.

Fitt 1

Hearken and listen, gentlemen
That be of freeborn blood.
I shall tell you of a yeoman good:
His name was Robin Hood.

Robin was an outlaw proud
While he walked upon the ground.
So courteous a one as he
Has never yet been found.

Robin once in Barnsdale stood
Leaning against a tree.
Beside him there stood Little John:
A yeoman good was he.

Much and Scathlock were standing there
(The miller was Much's sire).
Each little inch of doughty Much
Equalled a man entire.

And then suggested Little John
To noble Robin Hood,
"Master, if you would dine quite soon,
It would do you much good."

Then Robin Hood him answered back,
"To dine I have no wish

Until some unknown guest or lord
Is here to share my dish.

"Until some baron bold is here
Who may pay for the best
Or else some knight or travelling squire
That dwells off to the west."

Now Robin had a manor good
In the country where dwelt he.
Every day, before he dined,
He would hear Masses three.

Honouring the Father was the first,
The next, the Holy Ghost.
The third was for Our Lady dear
For her he loved the most.

"Master," then Little John intoned,
"So we on food can feed
Tell us which way we shall traverse
And do what sort of deed.

"Where shall we take, where shall we lead,
Where shall we lurk behind?
Where shall we rob, where shall we rieve,
Where shall we beat or bind?"

"It matters not," then Robin said.
"Good pickings will be found;
But look you do no farmer harm
That ploughs his piece of ground.

Nor shall you rob from yeoman good
That does in greenwood go
And neither harm a knight or squire

That would be a good fellow.

"These bishops and these archbishops,
These you shall beat and bind.
The High Sheriff of Nottingham,
Likewise hold him in mind."

"We will obey," said Little John.
"Your words won't be ignored.
'Tis late today God sends a guest
To join us at our board."

"Take then your good bow in your hand
And let Much go follow free
And so shall William Scathelock
And linger none with me.

"And get you going to the Sayles
And then to Watling Street
And wait until some guest unknown
You then may chance to meet.

"Be he an earl or baron bold,
Abbot or any knight,
Bring him ye to lodge with me
For a dinner fashioned right."

So upwards went they to the Sayles,
These stalwart yeomen three
And they looked east and they looked west,
But they could no man see.

But as they gazed from Barnsdale wood
In a place where none could see,
There came towards them a knight on horse.
They went to meet with he.

All dreary was his attitude
And little was his pride.
His one foot in the stirrup stood,
The other waved beside.

His hanging hood his eyes concealed.
Simple was his array.
A sorrier man than he was one
Rode never in summer's day.

Little John showed courtesy
And set him on his knee.
"O, welcome are you, gentle knight.
Welcome are you to me.

"Welcome are you to the greenwood,
O gracious knight and free.
My master for you has fasting stayed
No less than hours long three."

"Who is your master?" asked the knight.
John then said, "Robin Hood."
"He's a good yeoman," said the knight.
"Of him I've heard much good.

"Willingly will I go with you
Brothers in company.
At Blythe or Doncaster I'd have dined
Had you not met with me."

Onward then went this gentle knight.
Sad looks his face supplies,
While down his cheeks the tears they rolled
That spurted from his eyes.

They brought him to the lodge's door
And Robin did him see.
In courtesy he doffed his hood
And set him on his knee.

"Welcome, sir knight," then Robin said,
"Welcome are you to me.
I've waited for you, fasting, sir,
All of these past hours three."

And then replied the gentle knight,
With words both fair and free,
"God save you, worthy Robin Hood,
And all your company."

Together they wined and dined themselves
And on their meal set to.
Of bread and wine they had enough
And of deer's innards too.

Of waterfowl there was no lack,
Of pheasant and of swan,
And even of the little birds
That leafy twigs perched on.

"Eat well!" exhorted Robin Hood.
"I thank you, sir," said he.
"For such a dinner had I not
In all the past weeks three.

"If I come again, good Robin Hood,
Here in this green countree,
As good a dinner I shall make
As you have made for me."

"I thank you, knight," said Robin Hood,

"That dinner have I got.
By God, I ne'er so hungry felt,
Wishing to eat the lot.

"But pay before you go," said he,
"For it is only right.
It never was done, by God I swear,
For a yeoman to pay for a knight.

"No money have I," said the knight,
"That I may give for pay."
"Now, Little John, go have a look,"
Said Robin. "Don't delay."

"Tell me the truth," said Robin Hood,
"As God has part of ye."
"Than half a pound I have no more,
As God is part of me."

"If you've no more," said Robin Hood,
"I'll take no cash, it's true.
If you have need of any more,
More shall I lend to you."

Then Little John his mantle spread
Full fair upon the ground
And in the good knight's money box
Was only half a pound.

Little John let it stilly lie
And to his master fared.
"What tidings, John?" asked Robin Hood.
"He has the truth declared."

"Fill of the best wine," Robin said.
"The knight he shall begin.

Greatly surprised am I, sir knight,
Your clothing is so thin.

"Tell me one word," said Robin Hood.
"In confidence it shall be.
I'd guess you were a knight by force   *i.e., one*
virtually conscripted into knighthood
Or sprung from yeomanry.

"Or else you've been a sorry soul
And lived in stroke and strife,
A usurer or lecher vile
Leading a wrongful life."

"I am none of them!" proclaimed the knight,
"By God who fashioned me.
A hundred years there have been knights
Among my ancestry.

"But, often, Robin, has it chanced
Life may a man disgrace,
But God, who sits in heaven above,
Restores him to his place.

"But two or three years gone, Robin,
My neighbours understood
Four hundred pounds of wherewithal
I might spend as I would.

"And now bereft of all am I,
But my children and my wife
And this God has decreed, Robin,
Till he gives back my other life."

"In what way then," said Robin Hood,

"Did your riches from you flee?"
"It was all due to foolishness
And kindness done by me.

"I had a son, good Robin Hood.
As my heir he was then held.
When he was twenty winters old,
He at the joust excelled.

"He slew a knight of Lancashire.
He slew a squire so bold
And so to save his very life
Away my goods were sold.

"Collateral my lands became
Until a certain day
To the Abbot of St Mary's rich
To ensure that I would pay."

"What is the sum?" asked Robin Hood.
"Tell now the truth to me."
"Good sir, it was four hundred pounds
That he Abbot lent to me."

Asked Robin, "If you lose your land,
What then would your fate be?"
"Away I'd quickly take myself
Over the salty sea.

"And see where Christ was live and dead
On the mount of Calvary.
Farewell, my friend. Good day to you.
It may no better be."

The tears they rained from both his eyes.
He would have gone away.

"Farewll, my friend. Good day," he cried.
"I have no more to pay."

"Where are your friends?" then Robin asked.
"Good sir, they know me not.
When I was rich enough at home,
Of friends I had a lot.

"And now they run away from me,
Like beasts all in a row.
They take no heed of me indeed,
Because they scorn me so."

For pity then wept Little John,
Much and Scathlock with many a tear.
"Fill of the best wine," Robin said,
"For here is simple cheer."

"Have you any friends," good Robin asked,
"To be your security?"
"Alas! I've none," then said the knight,
"But God that died on the tree."

"O, trifle not," said Robin Hood.
"Of that I will have none.
Do you think I'd use God's guarantee,
Or Peter, Paul of John?

"No, no, by him who fashioned me
And formed both moon and sun,
Find me another surety
Or money you'll have none."

"I have none other," said the knight.
"It is the truth, I say.
Except for Our dear Lady who

Ne'er failed me to this day."

"By dear worthy God," said Robin,
"If I searched all England for
Security, I'd never find
A better guarantor.

"And now come hither, Little John,
And go to my treasury
And bring to me four hundred pounds
Counted accurately."

Over then went Little John
And Scathelock went before.
He counted out four hundred pounds
By eight and twenty score   *Little John proves*
over-generous in his calculations.

"Should this be done?" asked little Much.
John said, "Why shouldn't it be?
It's alms to help a gentle knight
Fallen in poverty."

"Master," then said Little John,
"His clothing's very thin.
You might give the knight a livery
To wrap his body in.

"For you have scarlet and green, master,
And many a rich array.
There is no merchant in merry England
So rich I dare well say."

"Take him three yards of every hue.
Well measured must it be."
His bow was Little John's yardstick.

No other needed he.

And of every handful that he took
An extra three feet took he.
"What devilkins draper," asked little Much,
"Do you take yourself to be?"

Scathlock stood full still and laughed,
"By God so full of might,
John may give him the better measure.
By God, it cost him light."

"Master," then said Little John
To gentle Robin Hood,
"You must give that poor knight a horse
To lead him home for good."

"A good grey courser take to him,
Also a saddle new.
He is Our Lady's messenger.
God grant that he be true.

"And a good palfrey," said little Much,
"To keep his status right."
"And a pair of boots," said Scathelock,
"For he is a gentle knight."

"What shall you give him, Little John?"
Asked Robin. "Gilt spurs two
To pray for all this company,
God his ordeal bring him through."

"When shall I pay you?" asked the knight.
"When wish you it to be?"
"This day twelve months," said Robin Hood,
"Under the greenwood tree."

"It is a great shame," Robin said,
"A knight alone to ride,
No squire, no yeoman or no page
To amble at his side.

"I'll lend you Little John, my man,
Your servant his estate
.Your yeoman's place he'll occupy,
If your need of him is great."

Fitt 2

Now is the knight gone on his way,
Thinking his fortune good.
When Barnsdale forest he perceived
He blessed good Robin Hood.

And when he thought on Barnsdale green,
On Scathlock, Much and John,
He blest them for the best of groups
He'd ever come upon.

And then the gentle knight spoke up.
To Little John said he,
"Tomorrow to York town must I go,
To St Mary's Abbey.

"And to the Abbot of that place
Four hundred pounds I'll hand
And, if I fail to do this act,
I'll forfeit all my land."

The Abbot all his monks addressed
There standing on the ground.
"A year ago there came a knight

And borrowed four hundred pound.

"Four hundred pounds he borrowed then,
His land for security,
But if he does not come today
Disinherited shall he be."

"The day is young," the Prior said.
"The day is early yet.
I'd rather pay a hundred pounds
And the whole thing forget.

"The knight is far beyond the sea.
In England is his right.
He suffers hunger, suffers cold
And many a sorry night.

"A pity 'tis," the Prior said,
"To take his land this way,
Your conscience is so light that you
Can cause him such dismay."

"Oh, you are always in my beard,"
Cried the Abbot. "God knows that."
The High Cellerer then strode up,
A monk whose head was fat.

"He's dead or hanged," proclaimed the monk,
"By God that bought me dear
And we shall have an income of
Four hundred pounds a year."

The Abbot and High Cellerer
Were standing full of pride
And the Justice, England's magistrate
Was on the Abbot's side.

The High Justice and many more
Held in their hand most strong
The whole debt that the poor knight owed
To put that knight to wrong.

They harshly judged the hapless knight,
The Abbot and company.
"Unless he comes here on this day,
Disinherited shall he be."

"He will not come," the Justice said.
"I daresay I am right."
But, in a moment sad for them,
To the gate there came the knight.

And then spoke up the gentle knight
To all his company.
"Now don your simple apparel   *To hide his new found fortune, the knight makes*
You brought for them to see."   *his followers put on shabby clothes.*

So they put on their simple clothes
And to the gates they strode.
The porter welcomed everyone
Who'd travelled by that road.

"Welcome, sir knight," the porter said.
"My lord's at dinner, true,
And with him many gentlemen
All waiting there for you."

The porter swore a mighty oath,
"By God that fashioned me,
Here is the finest muscled horse

I ever yet did see."

He said, "Them to the stables bring,
To settle comfortably."
"They shall not go there." said the knight,
"By God that died on a tree."

The lords were sat at their repast
There in the Abbot's hall.
The knight went forward and knelt down
Anf greeting gave them all.

"Please note, sir Abbot," said the knight,
"I'm here on the promised day."
The first word that the Abbot spoke
Was, "Have you got my pay?"

"No, not one penny," said the knight,
"By God who fashioned me."
"You're a debtor shrewd," the Abbot said.
"Good Justice, drink to me."

"Why are you here?" the Abbot cried,
"When you've not brought my pay?"
"For an extension," said the knight,
"Until some later day."

"Your day is done," the Justice said,
"Forever your land goes."
"Now, good sir Justice, be my friend.
"Protect me from my foes."

"But I am to the Abbot bound,
Bound both with cloth and fee." *This alludes*
to a medieval legal practice.
"Now, good sir Sheriff, be my friend."

"In God's name no," said he.

"Now, good sir Abbot, be my friend,
For all your courtesy.
Until I can reclaim my lands,
Hold them in hand for me.

"And I will be your servant true
And serve you faithfully
Till you have my four hundred pounds
Of money good and free."

The Abbot swore a mighty oath,
"By God who died on a tree,
Go get you land wheree'er you may,
For you'll get none for me."

"By worthy God," then said the knight,
"That all of this world wrought,
If ever I've my land again,
Dearly shall it be bought.

"God who was of maiden born
Allow me to succeed,
For it is good to have a friend,
If such a man have need."

The Abbot loathly looked on him
And evilly did call,
"You knight that's false, get out of here!
Go, hurry from my hall."

"You lie!" then said the gentle knight.   *The knight is outraged by the charge of false*
"Here, Abbot, in your hall,   *conduct.*
For a false knight I never was,

By God that made us all."

At once stood up that gentle knight.
To the Abbot mouthed he,
"To suffer a knight to kneel so long
Shows you've no courtesy.

"In jousting and in tournament
I frequently have been
And I've in peril put myself
As great as any seen."

"What extra money will you give,"   *The Justice suggests*
Asked the Justice, "for his land   *the Abbot should give the*
Or, Abbot, else you'll safely never   *knight a final payoff*
Hold it in your hand."   *to secure title.*

"A hundred pounds," the Abbot said.
Said the Justice, "Give him two."
"You'll not so get it," said the knight.
"Never, by God, will you."

He started towards the table then,
Up to the table round
And there he shook out of a bag
The whole four hundred pound.

"Here is your gold, sir Abbot,
Which you did lend to me.
Had you been courteous when I came
Rewarded you would be."

The Abbot sat and ate no more
For all his royal fare.

His head upon his shoulder sank.
He fast began to stare.

"Now, give me back my gold," he said,
"Sir Justice, that I gave you."
"No, not a penny," he replied,
And swore that this was true.

"Sir Abbot and you men of law,
Now have I held my day.
Now I shall have my land again
Whatever you can say."

The knight he started for the door.
Away was all his care
And on he put his clothing good.
The other left he there.

Out went he, on his lips a song,
As men have told the tale.
His lady met him at the gate
At home is Verysdale.   *Variant*
reading: Uterysdale.

"Welcome, my lord," his lady said.
"Is our land gone away?"
"Be merry dame," replied the knight.
"For Robin Hood you pray

"That ever his soul be in bliss.
He helped me in my need,
For, had he not his kindness shown,
Beggars we'd be indeed.

"The Abbot's claim I settled have.
He is served of his pay.

The yeoman good he lent it me
As I came by the way."

This knight lived happily at home,
It is the truth I say,
Till he had got four hundred pounds
All ready for to pay. *It was now time to
repay Robin the £400.*

He purchased him a hundred bows.
Whose strings were firm and tight,
A hundred sheaves of arrows good,
The heads all polished bright.

Each arrow was an ell in length
With peacock feathers bright,
Embellished all with silver they –
It was a seemly sight.

He brought with him a hundred men,
At that time clothed bright
And he himself in that same group
Was garbed in red and white.

He bore a stout lance in his hand
And a man brought his mail.
He rode along with a light song
To the woodland of Barnsdale.

He saw some wrestling at a bridge.
For a while tarried he
And there were all the best yeomen
Of all the west countree.

A full fair game was there set up.

The prize, a bull of white,
A courser, too, caparisoned
With golden tackle bright.

A pair of gloves, a red-gold ring,
A pipe of wine, I say.
Whatever man triumphant was
The prize should bear away.

There was a yeoman in that place.
The most worthy was he,
But, as he was a stranger there,
They thought he killed should be.   *Villagers have never much liked outsiders.*

The knight felt pity for this man
In the place where he stood
And said he should not suffer harm
For love of Robin Hood.

The knight then pressed into the place.
A hundred followed free,
With bows all bent and arrows sharp
To shame that company.

Shouldering all, they gave him room
To hear what he might say.
He took the yeoman by the hand
And gave him all the play.

He gave him five marks for his wine.
There it lay on the ground.
And said it should be given out
To all who came around.

So stayed the knight till play was done

And left it none too soon,
For, waiting, Robin fasting was
Three hours after the noon.

Fitt 3

[*We now join Little John, to learn of his adventures after he departed with Sir Richard, but before the latter returned to repay Robin*].

Now, listen, goodly gentlemen,
All you now gathered near.
Of Little John who served the knight
Good mirth you now shall hear.

It was upon a merry day
Young men would shooting go
And Little John said he would join
Them with his trusty bow.

Three times he shot and cleft the wand,
Which Nottingham's Sheriff saw,
For near the marks the Sheriff stood
And he was filled with awe.

The Sheriff swore a mighty oath,
"By him that died on a tree,
This man he is the archer best
That ever I did see.

"Now, tell me true, my bright young man,
Your name now to my face
And in what country you were born
And where your dwelling place."

"In Holderness I first saw light

I was told by my dame.
At home I'm Reynold Greenleaf called.
At home that is my name."

"Now tell me, Reynold Greenleaf,
Will you come dwell with me?
Each twelvemonth I will hand to you#
Twenty marks in fee."

"I have a master," then said John.
"A courteous knight is he."
"If you from him permission get,
Far better will it be."

The Sheriff then got Little John
From the knight for twelve months long.
Immediately he gave to him
A horse both good and strong.

Now Little John's the Sheriff's man,
But he did plot indeed
The Sheriff he discomfit would,
If he could do such deed.

"God help me now," said Little John,
"And let it truly be
That I'm the worst of underlings
That ever yet had he."

And, on a Wednesday, it befell
The Sheriff hunting went
And Little John was left abed,
His time in slumber spent.
Therefore poor John no breakfast had
And midday was now gone.
"Sir steward, I entreat of you

Some food," said Little John.

"It is too long for Greenleaf bold
A-fasting for to be.
Therefore, I pray you, steward good,
My dinner give to me."

"No food or drink," the steward said,
"Till t'Sheriff's back in town."
"I'd swear to God," cried Little John,
"I'd like to crack your crown."

The butler was uncourteous.
He stood upon the floor.
He hastened to the buttery,
Where fast he shut the door.

John gave the butler such a rap
His back near broke in two.
He'd never be the same again,
That wan, his whole life through.

He kicked the door in with his foot.
It shattered well and fine
And there he greatly helped himself
To drink, both ale and wine.

"Since you'll not dine," said Little John,
"I shall with drink make free
And, tho' you live a hundred years,
You'll still remember me."

And Little John both ate and drank
As much as he could hold.
In the kitchen was the Sheriff's Cook,
A stout man he and bold.

"I swear to God," proclaimed the Cook,
"You think you are too fine
For one who in a household dwells
To ask this way to dine."   *Customarily, John should have awaited the Sheriff's return before eating.*
And then he walloped Little John;
He landed larrups three.
"Oh, I dare swear," said Little John,
"That those three blows please me.

"You are a bold and doughty man
As far as I can see.
Before I pass out of this place,
You'll better tested be."

Then Little John his good sword drew.
The Cook took his in hand
And neither thought to flee away,
But stiffly did they stand.

There they fiercely fought together.
Much ground they trod upon,
But neither could the other hurt,
Tho' half an hour was gone.

"I swear to God," said Little John,
"And I speak truthfully.
You are one of the best swordsmen
That ever I did see.

"If you could shoot as well with bow
I'd to the woods you bring.
Two clothing changes you each year

Upon your back could fling

And twenty marks good Robin Hood
Would give you every year."
"Put up your sword," then said the Cook.
"We'll go as mates from here."

And then he fed to Little John
The entrails of a doe.
Good bread they ate, good wine they drank
And had a good time so.

And when they both had drunken well,
Their troth they paused to plight
That they would be with Robin Hood
That selfsame day at night.

They sped them to the treasure house
Fast as they could have gone
And they kicked in the good steel locks,
The Cook and Little John.

They helped themselves to many things
And all that they might get.
The silver vessels, cups and spoons
They'd none of them forget.

Also they took of currency
Three hundred pounds and three
And hastened straight to Robin Hood
Under the greenwood tree.

"God save you now, my master dear,
And Christ you saved may see."
Then Robin said to Little John,
"Welcome you truly be.

"And also that strong yeoman bold
You bring 'neath the greenwood tree.
What news is there from Nottingham?
Little John, tell it me."

"You're greeted by the Sheriff proud
Who sent you here by me,
With silver vessels and his Cook
Three hundred pounds and three."

"To God I promise," Robin said,
"And to the Trinity,
It never was with his consent
This fortune came to me."

Little John at once thought up
A piece of trickery
And five miles through the forest sped
To do what we shall see.

Then he met with the Sheriff proud
Hunting with hound and horn.
Little John made a courtesy
Guileless as one newborn.

"Now God save you, my master dear,"
Little John made a bow.
"Reynold Greenleaf," the Sheriff said,
"Where have you been till now?"

"I have been in this greenwood wide.
A fair sight did I see.
It was one of the fairest sights
Ever espied by me.

"Yonder I saw a right fair hart.
His colour was of green
And with him seven score of deer.
That is what I have seen.

"His antlers are so sharp, master.
Sixty points at least I'd say.
I dared not shoot the beast for dread
He'd charge and would me slay."

"I swear to God," the Sheriff said,
"This sight I'd like to see."
"Then hurry that way, master dear
And come along with me."

The Sheriff rode and Little John
Afoot was fast and smart
And when they before Robin came
Said, "Here's the master hart."

The Sheriff stood as still as still.
A sorry man was he.
"Woe take you, Reynold Greenleaf.
You were treacherous to me."

"I swear to God," said Little John,
"Master, you speak not fair.
When I was in your house today,
No dinner got I there."

The Sheriff was to supper brought.
Sorrowful was his plight.
He saw his vessel on the board
And it was silver white.

"Be cheerful, now," said Robin Hood.

"Sheriff, for charity
And for the love of Little John
Your life preserved will be."

When they had supped and had supped well
And the time when daylight goes,
Robin commanded Little John,
"Take off the Sheriff's clothes.

"His tunic and his furry coat
All made of different shades
And in a mantle green him wrap,
The hue of forest glades."

Robin then told his strong young men
Under the greenwood tree
That in such garments would they lie
So the Sheriff might them see.

And all night long the Sheriff lay
In his breeches and his shirt,
As custom was in the greenwood,
Tho' it made his sides both hurt.

"Now, make good cheer," said Robin Hood,
"Sheriff, for charity.
This is the order of our lives
Under the greenwood tree."

"No harder order," he replied,
"In hermitage so drear.
For all of merry England's gold,
I'd dwell no longer here."

"Another twelvemonth," Robin said,
"You shall dwell here with me

And I'll teach you, O Sheriff proud,
An outlaw for to be."

"Rather than stay another night,
Robin, I beg you to
Cut off my head," the Sheriff said,
"And I'll forgive it you."

"O, let me go," the Sheriff said,
"For holy Charity
And I will be the best of friends
That ever you will see."

"Then you to me an oath will swear,"
Said Robin. "Raise your hand.
You shall no ambush lay for me
By water or by land.

"And, if you find a man of mine,
Either by night or day,
Upon your oath you'll swear to me
To help him as you may."

Now has the Sheriff sworn his oath
And headed off for good,
For he had seen all that he wished
Of life in the greenwood.

Fitt 4

The Sheriff was back in Nottingham,
Pleased that he was there.
And Robin and his merry men
Went to thr woodland fair.

"Shall we now dine?" asked Little John.　　*It is now the*
day on which the knight is due
Robin Hood said, "Nay,　　　　　　　　　*repay Robin.*
For I fear Our Lady angry is,
For she saent me not my pay."

"Don't worry, sir," said Little John.
"The sun has sunk not yet
And I daresay and safely swear
Your payment you will get."

"Take your bow in hand," said Robin,
"Take Much upon your way
And also William Scathelock.
Let neither with me stay.

"And go a-walking up to Sayles
And then to Watling Street
And linger for some unknown guest,
Whom you may chance to meet.

"Whether a messenger he be,
Or a man of mirth should come,
Or, if he be a man who's poor,
Of my goods he will have some."

Then off at once strode Little John,
Half grumpy, from the scene
And on him placed a fine good sword
Under a mantle green.

Then they betook them to the Sayles,
All of these yeomen three
And they looked east and they looked west,
But no man could they see.

But, as they looked in Barnsdale green
And lurked by the highway,
They soon made out two black-clad monks,
Each on a good palfrey.

And then there muttered Little John
To Much on the highway,
"Now, I'd be willing for to bet
These monks have brought our pay.

"Now, make glad cheer," said Little John.
"Prepare your bows of yew.
Ensure your hearts are strong and firm,
Your strings both good and true."

The monk had two and fifty men,
Pack horses seven strong.
So royally no bishop rides
The highways all along.

"My brothers," then said Little John,
"In number we're but three,
But, unless we bring them home to dine,
We dare not Robin see.

"Bend now your bows," said Little John,
"And, bunched together, stand.
The foremost monk his life and death
I hold within my hand.

"Stop now, churl monk," said Little John.
"Stop now and stilly stand,
For note by the dear worthy God
Your life is in my hand.

"And evil luck upon your head

There under your hat band.
Too long you've made our master wait
To dine, you understand."

"Who is your master?" asked the monk.
Little John said, "Robin Hood."
"He is a strong thief," said the monk.
"I've never heard he's good."

"You tell a lie!" cried Little John,
"And saying that you'll rue.
He is a yeoman of the wood.
To dine he's bidden you."

Much was now ready with a bolt.
His bow you could see bend.
He aimed his arrow at the monk,
Forcing him to descend.

And of the fifty-two young men,
They all have fled and gone,
Save for a groom and little page
To lead the horses on.

They brought the monk to the lodge door,
If he wished for this or no,
That he might speak with Robin Hood.
There he'd no wish to go.

Good Robin then his hood did doff,
When he the monk did see.
The monk his hood kept on his head:
He was less mannerly.

"He is a churl," said Little John.
"Ill-mannered boor be he."

"Use then no force," said Robin Hood.
"He knows no courtesy."

"How many men," asked Robin Hood,
"Had this monk, Little John?"
"Two and fifty when we met,
But many of them are gone."

"Now, blow a horn," said Robin Hood,
"And our men summon so."
A hundred and forty yeomen tough
Came riding in a row.

And each one a good mantle wore,
Some striped and some were red
And they came to good Robin Hood
To listen to what he said.

They made the monk to wash and dry
And at his dinner sit.
Robin Hood and Little John
Themselves they both served it.

"Eat well, good monk," said Robin Hood.
"I thank you, sir," said he.
"Where is your abbey where you dwell.
Who can your patron be?"

"Saint Mary's Abbey," said the monk
And this he did aver.
"What is your office?" Robin asked.
"Sir, the High Cellerer."

"Then you're most welcome," Robin cried.
"On my luck I swear trulee.
Fill of the best wine," Robin said.

"This monk shall drink to me.

"But wonder fills me," Robin said.
"For all this lengthy day,
I feared Our Lady angry was,
For she sent not my pay."

"Have no doubt, sir," said Little John.
"You need not be so glum.
This monk has brought it, I dare say.
He's from her abbey come."

"She was a surety," Robin said,
"Between a knight and me
For a little money I him lent
Under the greenwood tree.

"And, if you have that silver brought,
I pray you let me see
And I shall help you any time,
If you have need of me."

The monk he swore a mighty oath
In accents sad and sore.
"Of the guarantee of which you speak
I never heard before."

"I swear to God," said Robin Hood,
"Monk, you are to blame,
For God is known for righteousness
As also is his dame.

"You told me this with your own tongue,
You cannot this deny,
That in her abbey you serve her
Each day that passes by.

"And you are made her messenger
My money for to pay
And therefore I more thankful am
That you are come today.

"What have you in your money box?"
Said Robin. "Truth tell me."
"Good sir," he answered, "twenty marks
And that is all there be."

"If that is all," said Robin Hood,
"I'll nothing take indeed
And I shall lend to you some more,
If any more you need.

"But if I find there's more," said he,
"It will be quickly taken
And all your coin of silvery shine
By you will be forsaken.

"Away with you now, Little John.
Find out the truth for me.
If there's no more than twenty marks,
None of it will I see."

Little John spread his mantle out
As he had done before
And counted the monk's wherewithal,
Eight hundred pounds and more.

Little John left it lying there
And to his master went.
"Our Lady now has sent to you
Double the cash you lent."

"I swear to God," said Robin Hood,
"Monk, tell me, what said I?
Our Lady is the truest woman
That ever I came by.

"By dear worthy God," said Robin,
"Though I searched all England for
A surety, I'd never find
A better guarantor.

"Fill of the best wine!" Robin cried.
"Toast now your Lady kind.
If she has need of Robin Hood,
A friend in him she'll find.

And, if she should more silver need,
Just come again to me
And by this token she has sent,
She shall have it times three."

The monk was going Londonwards
A gathering to meet
That he might the good knight cast down
And tread him under feet.

"Where are you off to?" Robin asked.
"To manors of this land
There with the bailiffs to confer,
As you may understand."

"Come over here, now, Little John,
And listen to my word.
A better one to search a monk,
Of him I've never heard.

"What's in the other money-box?

I think that we must see."
"Oh, by Our Lady," said the monk,
"You show no courtesy

"To bid a man to dinner come
And then him beat and bind."
"Our custom 'tis," said Robin Hood,
"To leave but little behind."

The monk spurred on his trusty horse.
No longer would he stay.
"Ah, have a drink," said Robin Hood,
"Before you ride away."

"In God's name, no," the monk replied,
Sorry he had come there.
"More cheaply I might well have dined
In Blythe or Doncaster."

"Greet well your Abbot," said Robin,
"And your Prior, too, I pray,
And bid them send me such a monk
To dinner every day."

Now we'll stop speaking of the monk
And we'll tell of the knight,
For yet he came to hold his day
While it was still daylight.

He sped him straight to Barnsdale wood
Under the greenwood tree
Where he found merry Robin Hood
And all his company.

The knight alighted from his steed
When Robin did him see.

O, courteously he doffed his hat
And set him on his knee.

"May God save you, good Robin Hood,
And all this company."
"Welcome are you, O gentle knight.
Welcome are you to me."

Then Robin Hood addressed the knight,
That knight who was so free.
"What need drives you to the green wood.
I pray, sir knight, tell me."

"Why took you so long, gentle knight?"
Asked Robin, accents bland.
"The Abbot and the Justice would
Have taken all my land."

"And have you now your land again?
Come, you must tell me true."
"I truly have it," said the knight,
"And I thank God and you.

"But angry do not be with me
Because I took so long.
I had to give a yeoman aid,
Else he'd have suffered wrong."

"In God's name, you must worry not,"
Said Robin. "Knight, attend.
Whoever helps a yeoman good,
I'll always be his friend."

The knight said, "Here's four hundred pounds,
The money you lent me
And here are also twenty marks

For your kind courtesy."

"In God's name, no," said Robin Hood.
"I need it not today,
For Our Lady by her cellarer
Has sent to me my pay.

"And, if I were to take it twice,
Shameful indeed 'twould be,
But truly, truly, gentle knight,
Welcome are you to me."

When Robin told the tale entire,
He laughed and had good cheer,
"But, by my truth," then said the knight,
"Your money's ready here."

"Employ it well," said Robin Hood,
"You gentle knight so free
And welcome be you, gentle knight,
Under my trystell tree.

"But what are all these bows for?
And these arrows feathered too?"
"By God," the knight replied to him,
"A present poor for you."

"Come here now to me, Little John.
Go to my treasury
And bring me the four hundred pounds
The monk o'erpaid to me.

"And have you here four hundred pounds,
You gentle knight and true,
And purchase horse and harness good
And gild your spurs anew.

"And, if you're ever short of coin,
Come visit Robin Hood
And, by my truth, I'll fail you not,
While I have any good.

"And use well your four hundred pounds,
Which once I lent to you
And keep yourself debt-free from now
And that's my counsel true."

So Robin Hood removed from him
That knight all of his care
And God that sits in Heaven high
Grant us all so well to fare.

Fitt 5.

Now bidden has the knight farewell
And gone upon his way.
Robin Hood and his merry men
Dwelled still for many a day.

Now, listen to me, gentlemen,
And listen carefully.
The Sheriff of Nottingham proclaimed
A contest of archery.

That all best archers of the north
Should come upon a day
And he that shot of all the best
The prize should bear away.

He that shot of all the best,
The best for all to see,
At a pair of targets finely made

Beneath the greenwood tree,

A right good arrow he would have,
The shaft of silver white,
The head and feathers rich red gold,
Truly, a unique sight.

Of this then heard good Robin Hood
Under his trystell tree.
"Prepare yourselves, you strong young men:
This shooting will I see."

"Now, hurry up, my merry men,
For you shall go with me
And I will test the Sheriff's faith
To see if true he be." *Robin wishes to test the Sheriff's promise not to molest the outlaws.*

When they had tested all their bows,
Their feathered tackle free
Seven score of strong young men
Stood by Robin's knee.

And when they came to Nottingham
They shot a distance long.
Many indeed the archers bold
Who shot with longbow strong.

"But six of you shall shoot with me.
The others guard to see,
Standing with their good bows bent,
That no one captures me."

Now three times Robin shot his bow.
The wand he always slit.

And Gilbert with the White Hand too
Three times the wand did split.

Little John and good Scathlock
Were archers good and free.
Reynold the good and little Much   *Here Reynold*
seems distinct from Little John.
Were not the worst to see.

And when they had all shot about,
Those archers fair and good,
Of every bowman who took part,
The best was Robin Hood.   *Huzzah!*

The silver arrow he received,
For worthiest was he.
They handed him the promised prize,
Which he took courteously.

Then they cried out, "It's Robin Hood!"
Great horns began to blow.
"We are betrayed," cried Robin Hood.
"True evil now we know.

"And woe to you, you Sheriff proud
For treating so your guest.
You promised otherwise to me
In yonder wild forest.

"But had I you in the greenwood
Under my trystell tree,
I'd get from you a better pledge
Than your true loyalty."

And many a longbow then was bent
And many an arrow flew

And many a tunic there was rent
That arrows had passed through.

The outlaws shot so mightily,
No man drove them away
And, as for the proud Sheriff's men,
They fled upon that day.

When Robin saw the ambuscade,
For the greenwood much yearned he.
Many an arrow there was shot   *It seems not all the*
Sheriff's men had fled.
Among that company.

Little John was sorely hurt
With an arrow in his knee
That he might neither run nor ride,
A very great pity.

"Master," then said Little John,
"If ever you love me
And for the love of that same Lord
Who died upon the tree

And, as reward for services
That I have rendered thee,
Do not allow the Sheriff to
Alive discover me.

"But draw you out your trusty sword
And then smite off my head.
No life allow to stay in me.
Make sure that I am dead."

"I don't want that," said Robin Hood,
"That, John, you should be slain,

Not if I all of England's gold
In recompense might gain."

"O, God forbid," said little Much,
"That died upon a tree,
That you should ever, Little John,
Part from our company."

He took him up upon his back
And carried him a mile,
Though many a time he laid him down
To shoot another while.

A castle fair there stood nearby
A little in the wood.
A double ditch it had about
With walls both stout and good.

And there there lived the gentle knight,
Sir Richard-atte-Lee,
Whom Robin Hood had given aid
Under the greenwood tree.

Inside he took good Robin Hood
And all his company.
"O, you are welcome, Robin Hood,
Welcome are you to me.

"I greatly thank you, Robin Hood,
For all your courtesy
And also for your kindness great
Under the greenwood tree.

"Of all the men who tread the earth,
None dearer is to me.
For all the Sheriff proud can do,

Secure here you will be.

"Now, shut the gates and draw the bridge
And hasten to the wall.
Prepare yourselves and arm yourselves
To guard the castle hall.

"But one thing I would, Robin, ask
And it is small: in fine
The twelve days that you stay with me   *How did he know Robin would stay only*
You'll sup and eat and dine."   *for twelve days?*

The table-cloths were swiftly spread,
The tables laid complete.
Robin and his merry men
Their food began to eat.

Fitt 6

Now, listen, all you gentlemen,
And hearken to your song,
How Nottingham's proud Sheriff came
And men with weapons strong

To the High Sheriff to get him   *For explanation see article 'High Sheriff'*
To rouse the country round
And they the castle of the knight
Did speedily surround.

The Sheriff loud began to cry
And said, "You traitor knight!
You harbour the King's enemy
Against the laws and right."

183

"Sir, I admit that I have done
The deeds proclaimed by you
Upon the lands that are my own,
As I am a knight true,

"So get you on your way and go
And do no more to me
Till you discover our King's will
And what that will might be."

The Sheriff so his answer had
Without any lying,
So he set off for London town
All for to tell the King.

And there he told him of the knight
And also Robin Hood
And also of the archers bold
That noble were and good.

"To rule the north with outlaws strong
And set yourself at nought,"
The Sheriff told the comely King,
"Is what he's always sought."

"I will arrive at Nottingham
Within the next fortnight
And I will capture Robin Hood,"
The King said, "and the knight.

"Now, home betake you, Sheriff proud,
And do as told by me:
Archers recruit in numbers good
From all the wide countree."

The Sheriff had set off for home
And went him on his way.
Robin returned to the greenwood
Upon a certain day.

When Little John was healed once more
Of the hole made in his knee,
He headed straight for Robin Hood
Under the greenwood tree.

And Robin in the forest walked
Under the leaves so green.
The Sheriff proud of Nottingham,
His sorrow could be seen,

Because he Robin could not catch.
He might not have his prey.
He sought to catch the gentle knight
By night time and by day.

Ever he sought the gentle knight,
Sir Richard-atte-Lee.
As he went to the riverside
To practise falconry,

He captured there the gentle knight
With men of arms so strong
And brought him back to Nottingham
All bound with rope and thong.

The Sheriff swore a mighty oath
By Him that died on a tree,
He'd rather than a hundred pound
That Robin his prisoner'd be.

Then the good lady, the knight's wife,

A lady fair and free,
She mounted on her palfrey good
And to the wood rode she.

When she came to the verdant wood
Under the greenwood tree,
She there discovered Robin Hood
And all his company.

"God save you, Robin Hood!" she said,
"And all your company.
I ask you for Our Lady's love
A favour grant to me.

"Do not allow my wedded lord
Shamefully slain to be,
For he is bound for Nottingham
And in captivity."

At once aloud cried Robin good
To that fair lady free,
"What man has captured your good lord?"
"The Sheriff proud," said she.

"The Sheriff proud has taken him –
It is the truth I say –
He can't be more than three miles gone
Along upon his way."

Like a madman up jumped Robin Hood
And forward then went he.
"Now, hurry up, my merry youths,
For Him that died on a tree.

"And anyone who does not come,
By Him that died on a tree

And Him who fashioned everything
No more shall dwell with me."

The outlaws with their bows set forth,
Seven score and more.
They pushed through hedge and leapt o'er ditch
Impeding them before.

"I vow to God," said Robin Hood,
"The knight I wish to see
And, if I can but rescue him,
Then will he be set free."

And when they came to Nottingham
And walked they in the street,
They saw ahead the Sheriff proud,
Whom they were soon to meet.

"Halt there, proud Sheriff," Robin said.
"Linger and speak with me.
I'd like some news about our king
Whom you have been to see.

"These seven years, by worthy God,
I have not hurried so
And I can swear, you Sheriff proud,
It is to cause you woe."

Robin bent then his trusty bow.
An arrow he let fly.
The Sheriff fell upon the ground.
It was his time to die.

Before the Sheriff could arise
Upon his feet to stand,
Robin chopped off the Sheriff's head

With the sword in his right hand.

"Now lie there dead, you Sheriff proud.
In the days when you did thrive,
There was no man who could you trust,
In the times you were alive."

His men drew out their shining swords,
That were so sharp and keen
And laid into the Sheriff's men
And drove them from the scene.

Robin went over to the knight.
His bonds he cut in two
And put into his hands a bow.
"An outlaw now are you.

"No more you'll gallop on a horse.
To run with Robin's men
You must within the greenwood learn,
Through mire and moss and fen.

For you shall come to the green wood
Where you shall hear birds sing
Till I forgiveness have procured
From Edward, our fair king.

Fitt 7.

The King arrived at Nottingham
With knights in great array
That he might prisoner Robin take
And the good knight, if he may.

He made enquiries round about
Concerning Robin Hood

And also of the gentle knight,
Who was so bold and good.

When they had told him of the case,
So the King would understand,
The latter quickly action took
And seized the good knight's land.

All the pass of Lancashire
He went both far and near
Until he came to Plumpton Park,
But found few of his deer.

Now, here, in days gone by, he'd seen
Many a herd of deer,
But now he hardly could find one
That bore good horns in here.

The King was furious at this
And swore by the Trinity,
"I would that I had Robin Hood
And with these eyes him see.

"And he who cuts off the knight's head
And brings it here to me,
He shall have all that knight's rich lands,
Sir Richard-atte-Lee

"I'll with a charter give it him
And seal it with my hand
To have and hold forever more
In all merry England."

Then up there spoke an aged knight,
Who was as true as day,
"O, listen, sovran lord and king,

To one word I shall say.

"There is no man dwells hereabouts
Would take Sir Richard's lands,
While Robin Hood is on the loose,
With his longbow in his hands.

"For he would lose his very head,
Let it be understood.
Give it no man, my lord the King,
That you wish any good."

For six months dwelt our comely King
In Nottingham and more,
Yet he could not find Robin Hood,
Which must have vexed him sore.

But always Robin rode about
By hiding place and hill
And always he the King's deer slew,
According to his will.

Then there spoke up a forester,
That stood by the King's knee,
"You must do what I will suggest,
If Robin Hood you'd see.

"Take five of the best knights you have.
Take them away from here
And dress them up in monkish garb.
As monks let them appear.

"Your cicerone I will be,
I'll guide you on your way.
Before you come to Nottingham,
My head as bet I'll lay

"That you will meet with Robin Hood,
If still alive is he.
Before you come to Nottingham,
Your eyes will Robin see."

Full hastily the King and knights
Donned habits merrily,
So just like monks they all appeared
To any who might see.

Our King had stiff boots on his feet.
It is the truth I say.
He singing rode to the green wood,
His party dressed in grey.

The horses that bore his supplies
Followed the King so free
Until at last they reached the wood
Of bosky greenery.

And there they met with Robin Hood
A-standing in the way
And so was many an archer bold.
It is the truth I say.

Now Robin held the monarch's horse.
He could no further ride.
And said, "Sir Abbot, by your leave,
A while must you abide.

"We yeomen of this forest are
Under the greenwood tree.
The King's deer form our provender,
For other have not we.

"Now you have churches, you have rents
And gold in great plenty.
Some of your money give to us
For holy charity.

And then spoke up our comely King
And this was what said he,
"I brought no more to the green wood
But forty pounds with me.

"In Nottingham I have been lodged
This fortnight with our King
And I have had to spend much cash
On many a great lording

And I have only forty pounds.
No more have I on me,
But if I had a hundred pounds
I'd give it you freely."

Robin took the forty pounds.
Into two split it he
And half gave to his merry men
And bade them merry be.

Then Robin courteously announced,
"Have this for your spending.
We're sure to meet another day."
"Thank you," replied our King.

"But Edward our king greets you well   *The King pretends*
to be his own messenger.
And sends his seal by me
And bids you come to Nottingham
For hospitality."

He then produced the royal seal,
Which he let Robin see
And courteously Robin Hood
He set him on his knee.

"I love no man in all the world
As well as our good King.
Welcome is your seal to me.
Likewise the news you bring.

"And, for the news you carry here,
Today you'll dine with me,
For love I bear my comely King
Under my trystell tree."

Onward by hand he led our King.
Forward the party fared
And many a deer was slain for meat
And quickly was prepared.

Robin took up a mighty horn
And long began to blow.
Seven score of strong young men
Approached them in a row.

And everyone knelt on his knee
Before good Robin Hood.
The King beneath his breath exclaimed
And swore by St Austin good,

"Indeed a wondrous sight is this,
Because I think I see
More loyalty his men bear him
Than any of mine bears me."

Their dinner ready quickly was

And off to it they'd gone.
They served our King with all their might,
Robin and Little John.

At once before our King was set
Meat on the table down,
The good white bread, the good red wine
And also fine ale brown.

"Now, make good cheer," said Robin Hood,
"Abbot, for charity
And for this happy piece of news,
You blessed more will be.

"Now shall you see what life we lead
Before you go from here
That you may tell our comely King
When 'fore him you appear."

Up jumped the merry men in haste.
Their bows they sharply bent.
The King feared he would soon be shot,
His clothes by arrows rent.

Two rods were by the men set up
As targets for the throng.
"By fifty paces," said the King,
"The distance is too long."

Each target a rose garland bore
'Neath which no shaft should fall.
"If any fail to strike the mark,"
Said Robin, "He must all

"His tackle hand over to me,
Even if it's fine,

For no man will I spare of this,
As I drink ale or wine.

"And he'll a buffet on his head   *For details of this game, see article 'Pluck buffet'.*
Receive," so Robin swore
And all who missed the garland gay,
He smote them wondrous sore.

Twice Robin took a shot himself.
Always the wand he cleft.
So Gilbert of the White Hand did.
He was an archer deft.

Little John and Scathlock good
Too low their arrows sped
And, when the garland gay they missed,
Robin sore struck each head.

And the last arrow Robin shot
Flew of the target wide.
He missed it by three fingers full
And somewhat more beside.

Then Gilbert with the White Hand spoke
And this is what he said,
"Master, your gear is lost and you
Must struck be on the head."

"If such be true," said Robin Hood,
"Then what must be must be.
Here are my arrows, abbot. Now
A buffet give to me."

"I'd rather not," the King replied,
"Good Robin, by your leave,

For, if a yeoman I should smite,
I fear it might him grieve."

"Now, clout me boldly," Robin said,
"For you have all my leave."
And then our King, on hearing this,
He soon rolled up his sleeve

And such a thwack he Robin gave,
He near fell to the ground.
"By God, a friar tough are you
That can land such a pound.

"There's muscle in your burly arm,
Which I will not forget."
This was how Robin and the King
There in the greenwood met.

Robin peered at our comely King
Intently in the face.　　　　　　　　　　*The penny drops.*
Robin recognises the king.
So did Sir Richard-atte-Lee
And knelt down in that place.

And so did all the outlaws wild
And they heard Robin tell.
"My lord the King of England,
Now do I know you well."

"Mercy!" then Robin asked the King.
"Under this trystell tree,
Grant of your goodness and your grace,
For all my men and me.

"Yes, in God's name," said Robin Hood,
"And also God me save!

For me and all my followers
Mercy I truly crave."

"Yes, in God's name," then said the King.
"Yes, I will grant your plea,
Provided that you leave the wood
And all your company.

"And come with me, sir, to my court:
There must you dwell with me."
And Robin made a vow to God
That right so should it be.

"I will come to your royal court
Your service for to see
And bring with me my merry men,
Seven score and three.

"But, though your service I will take,
I will come here once more
To shoot the brown deer of the wood,
As I have done before."

Fitt 8.

"Have you good green cloth?" asked our King,
"That you will sell to me?"
"Indeed, by God," said Robin Hood,
"Thirty yards and three."

Then to our hero said the King,
"Robin, a quantity
Of that same cloth I'd ask you sell
To my company and me."

"Indeed, by God," then Robin said,

"Else I would be a fool,
For you will give me livery
To wear when in comes Yule."

The King then cast from him his coat
And donned a garment green
And every knight was given one,
As could be clearly seen.

When they were dressed in Lincoln green,
They cast away their grey.
"Now shall we go to Nottingham,"
They heard King Edward say.

Their bows they bent and forth they went
A-shooting here and there
Towards the town of Nottingham,
Outlaws as they were.

And Robin with King Edward rode –
It is the truth I say –
They played pluck buffet as they shot
And they went by the way.

And many a buffet our King one
Of Robin Hood that day.
And Robin Hood did not hold back
When he struck the King in pay.

"So God help me," our King declared,
"I can't learn this game here.
I could not beat you with a shot
Though I shot all this year."

The townsfolk there in Nottingham,
In fear their blood congealed.

They saw a host in Lincoln green
That covered all the field.

Then every man said to his friend,
"In death I fear did fall
Our comely King and Robin Hood
Will massacre us all."

Hastily they began to flee.
They ran and no one stopped.
Old dames whose legs were rickety
Over their crutches hopped.

The King he gave a loud guffaw
And then himself revealed.
When everyone the King beheld
Their blood all uncongealed.

They ate and drank and made them glad
And sang with notes so free
And then our comely King addressed
Sir Richard-atte-Lee.

He gave him back his land again
And good told him to be.
Robin thanked his comely King
And set him on his knee.

Now Robin dwelt at the King's court
A dozen months and three.
He spent a hundred pounds, no less,
And all his followers' fee.

In every place that Robin came,
His money he laid down.
He spent on knight, he spent on squire

To get him great renown.

But when a full year had passed by
All of his men were gone
Except for two, Will Scathelock,
And also Little John.

As Robin saw some young men shoot
With talent one fine day,
He cried, "Alas! My money's gone!
My wealth has gone away.

"One time I was an archer good,
Accomplished, very strong,
Counted by all as England's best
By all men in the throng.

"Alas!" then said good Robin Hood.
"Alas and well a woo *This line is so*
comprehensible and so expressive, I
If I dwell longer with the King, *felt no need to*
modernise it.
I'll die of sorrow true."

So Robin Hood went forth at once
Till he came to our King.
"My lord," said he, "I've a request.
Grant me what I'm asking.

"In Barnsdale I a chapel built
That lovely is to see.
It is of Mary Magdalene
And there I wish to be.

"So much for the past seven nights
I could not sleep a wink

And for all these past seven days
I could not eat or drink.

"To go to Barnsdale I desire.
From it I cannot stay.
As a barefoot pilgrim, clad in wool,
There I must make my way."

"If it be so," then said our King,
"It may no better be.
I will permit you seven nights
To dwell away from me."

"I thank you, lord," said Robin Hood
And set him on his knee.
He took his leave full courteously.
To the greenwood, then, went he.

And when he to the greenwood came
In the merry morning,
He heard from branches little notes
That birds make as they sing.

"A long time's passed," said Robin Hood,
"Since last I wandered here.
I think I'd like to try my hand
At shooting the brown deer."

Robin slew a full great hart.
His horn then did he blow
So all the wolfsheads of the wood
Its merry notes would know.

The outlaws soon assembled were
Before much time could flow.
Seven score of strong young men

Came ready in a row.

The outlaws quickly doffed their hoods
And set them on their knee
And loudly welcomed Robin Hood
Under this greenwood tree.

So Robin in the greenwood dwelt
For twenty years and two.
For fear of Edward who was king
The court he did eschew.

And yet he suffered trickery
From a woman steeped in sin.
The Prioress of Kirklees she,
Who was of his near kin.

She was enamoured of a knight
And him she loved a lot.
Roger of Doncaster his name
And evil was their plot. *Their motive is obscure.*

They planned together how to slay
Our hero, Robin Hood,
A murderous deed to see what way
Accomplish it they could.

Then Robin Hood spoke up one day
In the green place where he stood.
"I must have my blood let," said he, *See article*
"Bloodletting"
"By the Prioress so good."

Sir Roger of Doncaster, knight,
By the Prioress lay he
And they betrayed good Robin Hood

Through their false treachery.

May Christ have mercy on his soul,
This wolfshead, Robin Hood,
An outlaw of benevolence,
Who did the poor much good.

Appendix

Robin Hood Ballads

Birth of Robin Hood
Little John and the Four Beggars
Robin Hood and Alan-a-Dale
Robin Hood and Guy of Gisborne
Robin Hood and Little John
Robin Hood and Maid Marian
Robin Hood and Queen Katherine
Robin Hood and the Beggar (title of two ballads)
Robin Hood and the Bishop
Robin Hood and the Bishop of Hereford
Robin Hood and the Butcher
Robin Hood and the Curtal Friar
Robin Hood and the Golden Arrow
Robin Hood and the Monk
Robin Hood and the Pedlars
Robin Hood and the Potter
Robin Hood and the Prince of Aragon
Robin Hood and the Ranger
Robin Hood and the Scotchman (two versions)
Robin Hood and the Shepherd
Robin Hood and the Tanner
Robin Hood and the Tinker
Robin Hood and the Valiant Knight
Robin Hood Newly Reviv'd
Robin Hood Rescuing the Widow's Three Sons
Robin Hood's Birth, Breeding, Valour and Marriage
Robin Hood's Chase
Robin Hood's Death
Robin Hood's Delight
Robin Hood's Golden Prize
Robin Hood's Golden Prize
Robin Hood's Progress to Nottingham

Robin Hood's Rescuing Will Stutely
The Bold Pedlar and Robin Hood
The Jolly Pindar of Wakefield
The King's Disguise and Friendship with Robin Hood
The Noble Fisherman

Longer Poetic Versions

A Little Gest of Robin Hood
A True Tale of Robin Hood (Martin Parker)
Bibliography

Bellamy, J. *Robin Hood: an Historical Enquiry* London, 1985
Bett, H. *English Myths and Legends* New York, 1991
Burgess, G. *Two Medieval Outlaws* Cambridge, 1997
Clarke, D. *Ghosts and Legends of the Peak District* Norwich, 1991
Clarke, D. *Strange South Yorkshire* Wilmslow, 1994
Clarke, D. *Supernatural Peak District* London, 2000
Cooper, A. and P. *William Wallace: Robin Hood Revealed* Greenock (Pa.), 2000
de Vries, R. *On the Trail of Robin Hood* Hightown, 1988
Dobson, R.B. and Taylor, J. *Rymes of Robin Hood* London, 1976
Doel, F. and G. *Robin Hood: Outlaw or Greenwood Myth?* Stroud, 2000
Eberhart, G.M. *Mysterious Creatures* Santa Barbara, 2002
Fitch, E.L. *In Search of Herne the Hunter* Chieveley, 1994
Gable, J.H. *Bibliography of Robin Hood* Lincoln (Nebraska), 1939
Green, B. *Secrets of the Grave* n.p., 2001

Green, B. *The Outlaw Robin Hood; his Yorkshire Legend* Huddersfield, 1991

Hahn. T. (ed.) *Robin Hood in Popular Culture* Cambridge 2000

Harris, P.V. *The Truth About Robin Hood* Mansfield, 1973

Hole, C. *English Folk-Heroes* London, 1948

Holt, J.C. *Robin Hood* London, 1991

Hulbert, M.F.H. *Little John of Hathersage* Hathersage, n.d.

Hutton, R. *The Rise and Fall of Merry England* Oxford, 1994

Jones, K.I. *Robin Hood in Cornwall* Penzance, 1997

Judge, R. *The Jack-in-the-Green* London, 2000

Keen, M. *The Outlaws of Medieval Legend* New York, 1989

Knight, S. *Robin Hood; a complete study of the English outlaw* Oxford, 1994

Lees, J. *The Legendary Exploits of Robin Hood* Nottingham, 1987

Lees, J. *The Quest for Robin Hood* Nottingham, 1987

Matthews, J. *Robin Hood, Lord of the Wildwood* Glastonbury, 1993

Mitchell, W.R. *The Haunts of Robin Hood* Clapham (Yorks.), 1970

Molyneux-Smith, T. *Robin Hood and the Lords of Wellow* Nottingham, 1998

Morrell, R.W. *Nottingham's Mysterious Mazes* Nottingham, 1990

Morrell, R.W. *Nottinghamshire Holy Wells* Nottingham, 1988.

Palmer, R. *Folklore of Gloucestershire* Stroud, 2001

Petry, M.J. *Herne the Hunter* Reading, 1972

Phillips, G. and Keatman, M. *Robin Hood: the Man Behind the Myth* London, 1995

Pickford, D. *Staffordshire: its Magic and Mystery* Wilmslow, 1996

Ralls-MacLeod, K. and Robertson, I. *The Quest for the Celtic Key* Edinburgh, 2002
Ritson, J. (ed.) *Robin Hood* London, 1823
Roberts, A. *Ghosts and Legends of Yorkshire* Norwich, 1992
Russell, B. and T. *Mysterious Kingston* Wimbledon, 1996
Rutherford-Moore, R. *Robin Hood: on the Outlaw Trail in Nottingham and Sherwood Forest* Chieveley, 2002
Rutherford-Moore, R. *The Legend of Robin Hood* Chieveley, 1998
Simek, R. *Dictionary of Northern Mythology* Cambridge, 1993
Simpson, J. and Roud, S. *The Oxford Dictionary of English Folklore* Oxford, 2000
Smith, G.K. *The Wizard, the Worms and Robin Hood* Edinburgh, 1994
The Robin Hood Walks Leicester, 1994
Westwood, J. *Albion* London, 1985
Wilson, S. *Robin Hood: the Spirit of the Forest* London, 1993

www.ingramcontent.com/pod-product-compliance
Lightning Source LLC
Chambersburg PA
CBHW022357040426
42450CB00005B/221